HOW DO WE DESIGN CLASSROOMS TO FIT THE NEEDS OF A DIVERSE POPULATION OF LEARNERS?

THIS BOOK IS FILLED WITH PRACTICAL STRATEGIES TO GET YOU STARTED!

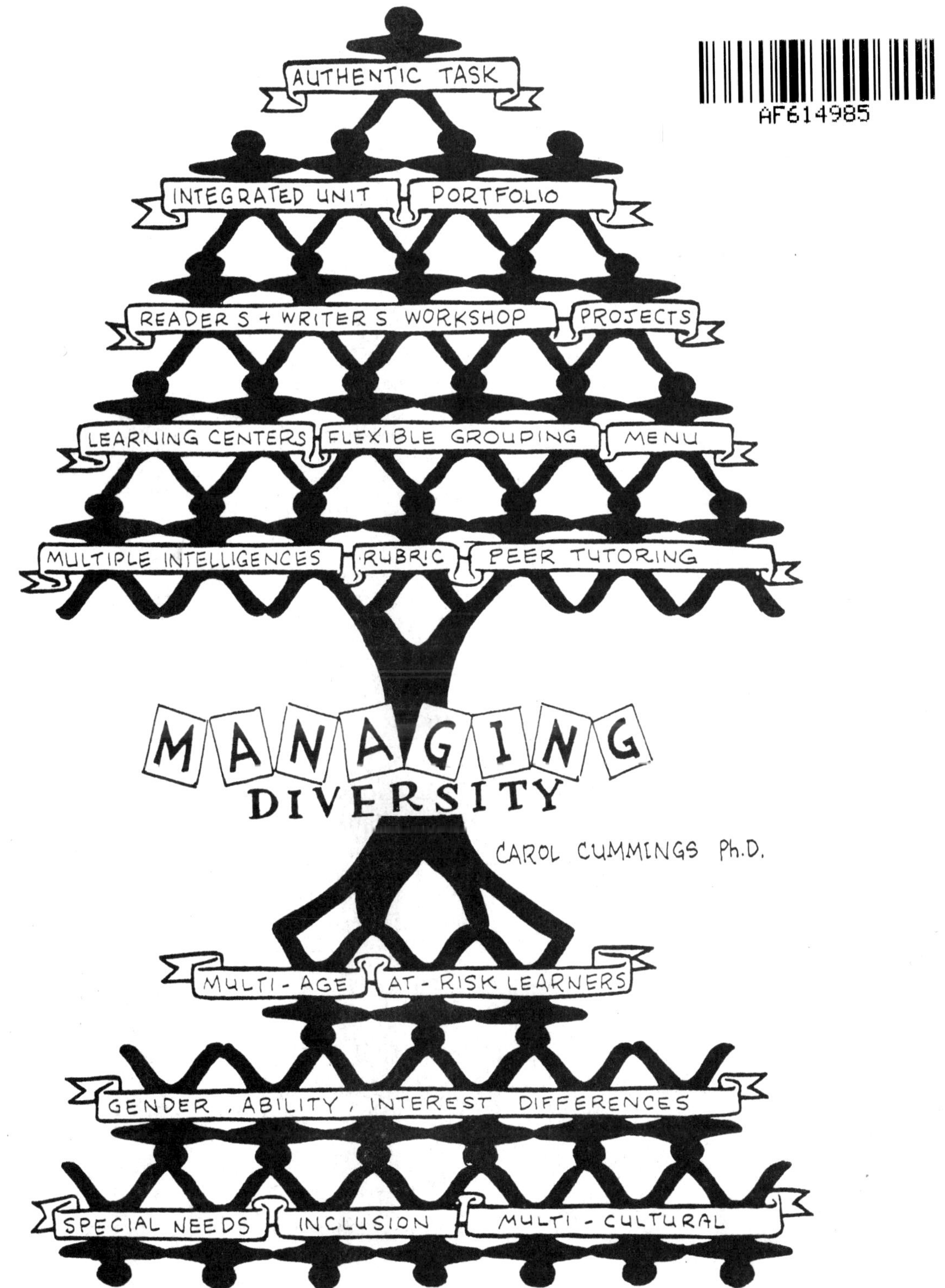

Published by TEACHING, INC.
P.O. Box 788
Edmonds, WA 98020
(206) 774-0755

ISBN 1-881660-03-6
$14.95

THIS BOOK WAS WRITTEN
FOR ALL OF THE TEACHERS
WHO CARE
TO TOUCH THE SOUL
OF EVERY CHILD.

The Unchild

I am the unchild
unwanted
unkempt
unloved
uneducated
uncaring
unfavored
unmotivated
unnoticed
unworthy
unprotected
unable to undo this
unnatural
undesirable
unnecessary
cycle of the UNCHILD
UNLESS
UNEXPECTANTLY AN
UNDERSTANDING
UNINHIBITED
UNDAUNTED
TEACHER
touches my soul.

poem written by Lucy Malacos, teacher, Saginaw, MI

TABLE OF CONTENTS

PLANNING FOR DIVERSITY

WHY CHANGE?

Ask yourself how this list of opposites relates to classroom teaching:

tall..........short
advantaged..........disadvantaged
lucky..........unlucky
healthy..........unhealthy
prepared..........unprepared
majority..........minority

Did you think, "Today's classroom is filled with opposites." Today's classroom *is* filled with diversity. The demands upon the teacher to meet the needs of all children have increased dramatically. The teaching model of the past worked for a more homogenous grouping of students. It doesn't work today. It would be criminal to keep 30 diverse students together, throughout the day, for lock-step teacher input and student practice. The goal of this book is to provide concrete, practical teaching strategies to improve the odds that all children in the diverse classroom have a chance to succeed. The premise of this book is that you believe all children:

- Have the right to succeed
- Deserve an opportunity for continuous progress
- Should not have to face academic failure at a young age

Accomplishing these goals *and* celebrating heterogeneity in gender, ability, interests, and age levels will require the use of:

- Integrated units
- A whole language approach
- Learning centers
- A developmental approach
- Individualized instruction
- Cooperative learning
- Authentic assessment
- Team planning

These exemplary strategies which are found in many classrooms today will be discussed in the following chapters. This book is a compilation of successful strategies the author has personally observed in classrooms from coast to coast.

A DAY AT A GLANCE

What might a day look like in a classroom where these strategies are in place? Sometimes students are working alone, sometimes in cooperative groups. Sometimes they are involved in a whole-class activity, and sometimes they receive direct instruction from the teacher. It wouldn't be unusual for this class to be involved in whole group science and social studies lessons, but receive individualized or small group math instruction.

The beginning and end of each day (home base time) involve a whole-class activity. For example, one class begins each morning writing in their journal in response to a prompt on the board. The teacher selects the prompt based on the social skill needs of the class. One such prompt reads, "Someone calls you a name on the playground. What are your choices?" After writing in their journals, students meet in small, heterogeneous groups to discuss their responses to the prompt.

After journal writing, three major blocks of time are scheduled:

BLOCK 1 = COMMUNICATION ARTS
BLOCK 2 = MATHEMATICS
BLOCK 3 = SOCIAL STUDIES/SCIENCE

These blocks may include time at learning centers and may also, as appropriate, be part of an integrated unit. Other studies and activities are built into the schedule, depending on whether students go to a specialist for instruction (for physical education or art—for example) or remain with the same teacher. It is easier to integrate such disciplines into learning centers, or the three blocks, when students remain with the same teacher (or team of teachers).

Sample Daily Schedule

Home base	**Block 1** (Communication Arts: reading, writing, etc.)	**Block 2** (Mathematics)	**Block 3** (Social studies-Science)	**Home base**
Social skills	*Journal*	*Individualized contracts, or math menu*	*Rotating units or projects*	*Self-evaluate*
Journal	*Trade books*	*Skill groups*	*Direct instruction*	*Learning log*
Goal setting	*Writing workshop*	*Direct instruction*	*Team activities*	
	Reading workshop	*Team activities*		
	Literature club			
	Direct instruction			
	Skill groups			

Learning centers may be incorporated into any of the scheduled blocks. For example, students may be at centers during the communication arts block while the teacher is working with small, skill-based groups.

WHAT TO TEACH

At the beginning of the school year, placement tests enable the teacher to develop flexible skill groups. Knowing where the students are conceptually also helps the teacher select learning experiences at the correct level of difficulty for the class. The tests, whether teacher made or commercial, should be easy to administer and score and should reflect a whole language, continuous progress philosophy. For example, below are three continua for reading, writing, and mathematics. A starting place for instruction can be determined by observing students ("kid watching"), studying their written composition, and listening to them read, as well as by scoring placement tests. The skillful teacher now has a scaffolding in place to allow students to advance at their own pace from one concept to the next.

DEVELOPMENTAL MILESTONES: READING

Student name								
Chooses to look at books								
Tells story by looking at pictures								
Uses left to right, top to bottom (directionality)								
Alphabet recognition—verbally and visually (when given randomly)								
Reads first/last name, familiar labels/signs								
Can match printed and spoken words one-to-one								
Uses beginning/ending/middle sounds to predict a word								
Develops a sight vocabulary								
Predicts word from another familiar word; recognizes syllables								
Begins to read fluently								
Self-corrects to "make sense"								
Reads with expression								
Retells story using problem, solution, setting, characters								
Reads independently (for pleasure and for information)								
Can skim a given selection for main ideas, plot, etc.								
Can scan text for particular information								
Monitors self while reading; uses "fix-up" strategies when necessary								
Uses a variety of strategies spontaneously (e.g., prereading)								
Views self as a reader; spends quality time reading								

Continue to add developmental steps to this continuum.

DEVELOPMENTAL MILESTONES: WRITING

Student name								
Uses scribbling, drawing to communicate								
Describes drawing w/dictation								
Scribbling includes letters								
Sound/symbol correspondence shown via invented spelling								
Words include beginning, middle, ending sounds								
Begins to use vowels as place holders								
Begins to write in sentences								
Predictably uses vowels as place holders in words								
Conventional spelling evident								
Begins to write using paragraphs								
Punctuation evident (periods, capitals, etc.)								
Can tell a story in writing (problem, solution, characters, setting)								
Demonstrates steps in process writing: • can generate ideas for writing; purposes for writing • revises to improve word choice, organization • edits to eliminate errors • shares writings								
Can write • a narrative • an expository paper • an explanatory paper • a descriptive paper • a persuasive paper								
Uses dialogue effectively								

Continue to add developmental steps to this continuum.

DEVELOPMENTAL MILESTONES: MATHEMATICS

Student name								
Counts aloud								
Shows one to one correspondence with objects								
Can match numeral with set								
Can distinguish greater than and lesser than								
Demonstrates addition and subtraction								
Can count to 100								
Can count by 2, 5, 10...								
Can measure using both standard and nonstandard measures								
Can explain graphs (bar, circle, picture)								
Can explain simple fractions								
Shows understanding of time (hours—minutes)								
Shows understanding of place value								
Can construct a graph								
Demonstrates multiplication and division								
Can interpret simple equations								

Continue to add developmental steps to this continuum.

PARENT INTERVIEWS

In addition to assessing where learners are intellectually, interview parents to find out more about the student personally. Include a simple survey in the letter you send home at the beginning of the year. Or, better yet, send the survey before the school year begins. Ask parents to describe their child's:

- Interests
- Strengths
- Special needs
- Favorite activities
- Reading and writing choices
- Learning style preferences

FORMING GROUPS

Having diagnosed students both cognitively and affectively, the teacher can select learning opportunities and decide what types of groups to form. Grouping decisions may be based on the student's need, interests, or learning style. In fact, the sample daily schedule provided earlier cannot be developed until we've first diagnosed our students. After all, *we teach children, not subjects!*

MULTI-AGE CLASSROOMS

A multi-age classroom may make it easier to provide a continuous progress program for a diverse population, but it is *NOT* absolutely necessary. Here are just a few of the pros and cons of multi-age groupings:

PROS

- Keeping the same students for more than one year eliminates the "getting to know you" and diagnosing academic strengths each September. Predictability and routines, so important for at-risk learners, are established and maintained over a longer period of time. The period of time spent teaching a management system in a graded system, the first three to four weeks of school, is minimized in the second year of a multi-age grouping. The returning one-half of the students teach the newcomers how the system works! Rituals and traditions are characteristic of this family-like grouping. Students are heard saying, "...but aren't we going to do that again this year?"

- It's easier to celebrate learning at different rates and levels than to think of a student as "second grade" and compare that child's progress to the "second-grade curriculum."
- Peer tutoring is facilitated. A nine-year old sitting at a table with a seven-year-old provides help naturally. The beauty of this arrangement is that perhaps next year the seven-year old (then eight) becomes the tutor.
- When students are given two or three years to demonstrate achievement, more of them experience success.
- Multi-age classrooms minimize retention in grade. Retained children actually perform more poorly on average when they go on to the next grade then if they had been promoted without repeating a grade. (Slavin & Madden, 1989)

The Society for Developmental Education (1993) has a motto: Childhood should be a journey, not a race. Their "Children's Bill of Rights" (developed by J. Grant) proposes that every child has the right to...

Attend a continuous progress program.
The continuity of having a teacher for more than one year.
Experience continual learning success.
Take an extra year in a multiage program without the stigma of school failure.
Be free from tracking.
Learn in a developmentally appropriate program.
Learn in a heterogeneous classroom.
Learn in a whole language classroom.
Learn in a cooperative learning classroom.
Be evaluated with authentic assessment tools.

Note that although a multi-age structure makes the "Children's Bill of Rights" easier to implement, it is not absolutely necessary. The continuity of having a teacher for more than one year can be accomplished using *looping*—a teacher stays with the same group of students from one year to the next (i.e., a class stays together and has the same teacher for two years in a row).

Today's classrooms are more heterogeneous than ever before in the history of education. A multi-age setting further increases the diversity. With skillful teaching and careful planning, it is possible, though, to provide everything mentioned in the "Children's Bill of Rights" in the "graded classroom."

CONS

- District policies may not keep pace with the changes taking place within the classroom. For example, administering grade level standardized assessment tests sets up a comparative/competitive evaluation system. This is counter productive to a continuous progress program using authentic assessment measures. Eliminating an ABCD marking system, eliminating tracking, and eliminating retention in grade are prerequisites to ungradedness.
- The parents and the community may not be adequately prepared for this change.
- Teachers may not be philosophically ready for the change nor adequately trained in nongraded practices.
- The research base supporting nongradedness is fairly old (1968-1976). There is a need for newer studies based upon today's population of students (Anderson & Pavan, 1993).

SUMMARY

To meet the needs of today's diverse population of learners will be a challenge to even the most motivated of teachers. As Henry Ford once said, "Whether you think you can or think you can't, you're right." We hope this book will convince you, *you can!* This chapter focused upon diagnosing your learners and rethinking your schedule in terms of major blocks of time.

CHAPTER 2

INTEGRATED, THEMATIC UNITS

Do these emerging trends sound familiar to you: developmentally appropriate practice (DAP), literature based, whole language, authentic tasks, performance assessment, and interdisciplinary teaching? In the move to restructure schools, these are but a few of the changes or concepts proposed. While the purpose of this book is to manage teaching in a diverse classroom—whether it's multi-age, multi-cultural, or multi-needs (i.e. inclusion)—many of the changes proposed for restructuring are basic to the organization and operation of a diverse classroom.

Implementing these trends sounds overwhelming! Where do you begin? For the purposes of this book, the integrated, thematic unit will be the organizing hub. In this chapter, we'll look at how to develop a thematic unit.

DEVELOPING A THEMATIC UNIT

- Select the theme.
- Integrate the theme by webbing the connections.
- Ask guiding questions to make the unit interdisciplinary.
- Align the unit with district standards or benchmarks for promotion.
- Develop authentic tasks to measure accomplishment.

WHY INTEGRATE?

Have you ever felt totally fragmented by the end of the year? Felt as if you hadn't been able to teach all of the objectives or content you were expected to teach? Did you feel overloaded? In fact, do you think each year the district adds more content for you to teach and at the same time doesn't give you the extra time or training to do it? Thematic units help reduce that fragmentation and also reallocate your time; not add time, but reallocate how you teach and what you teach.

Brain researchers (Caine & Caine, 1991) argue that teachers need to maximize learning by *providing interconnectedness.* The brain seeks patterns; it looks for meaning. Think about how easy it is to remember a rhyme, a poem, or a song, as compared to an isolated fact. The pattern within the poem or the song is much more predictable and meaningful. In fact, our brains will remember more information in the context of a pattern or a larger frame of reference. A thematic unit provides a wider frame of reference. A theme is a wide-angle lens through which to view the content we teach (Perkins, 1989).

Imagine the thematic unit as the hub and the elements of restructuring as the spokes.

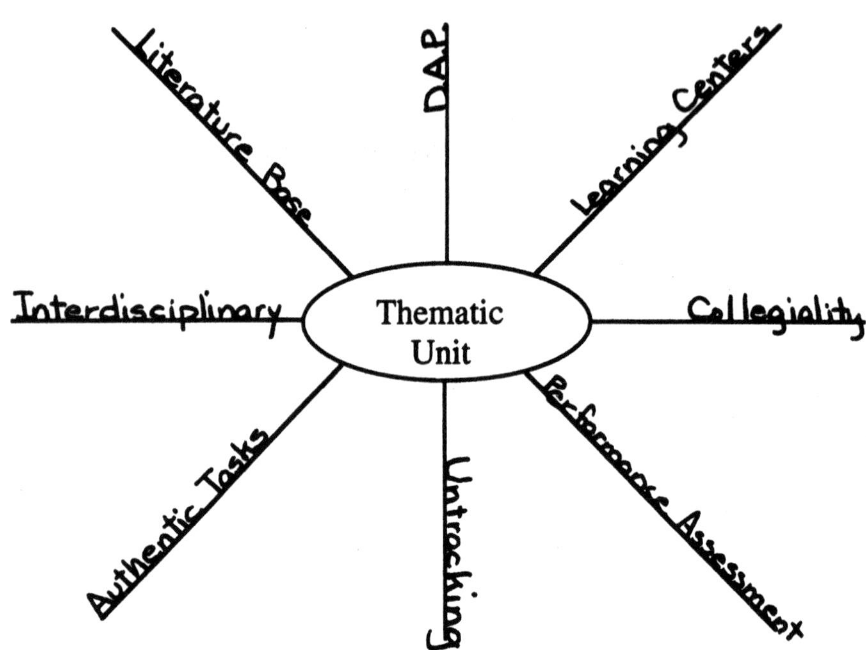

LEARNING CENTERS

Learning centers are a vehicle to provide developmentally appropriate practices in the elementary grades. Centers can be designed to address the two dimensions of developmental appropriateness, *age* and *individual* appropriateness. Centers provide activities that are concrete and real to children, while the thematic unit guides the selection of those activities.

LITERATURE BASED

Fragmentation is reduced when we let social studies and science curricula guide us in our selection of activities for the communication arts component. Our reading selection, our writing activities, and our speaking and listening opportunities can be driven by the content in the social studies and science objectives. It seems only natural that when the theme is *relationships*, and the social studies curriculum includes a unit on family and pets, that the books children read and their writing experiences should center around family relationships and pets. Immersing children in reading and writing activities that fit naturally with social studies and science curricula is an example of optimal time management. Using strategies like reading workshop and writing workshop accommodates the range of skill levels within diverse classrooms.

COLLEGIALITY

In the intermediate grades, teachers often separate into departments. Whether they teach in multi-age or graded classrooms, a thematic unit will help them focus the planning they do together. We call this *parallel* planning, as the teachers plan together, bring their units together through a common theme or topic. Bringing teachers together into a team fosters collegiality and movement toward restructuring.

PERFORMANCE ASSESSMENT/AUTHENTIC TASKS

One element of restructuring is movement away from using narrowly defined behavioral objectives to assess students toward using authentic tasks to assess performance. A thematic unit helps us design authentic tasks by linking the disciplines with coherent and meaningful connections.

SELECTING A THEME

Charles F. Kettering once said, "A problem well stated is a problem half solved." This is ever so true with the selection of a theme for your unit. In selecting a theme, look for an organizing concept. Perkins (1989) suggests you ask yourself:

- Is this a powerful idea that helps students see their world in more connected ways?
- Does the theme have "real world" application?

- Does this theme cut across the disciplines (does it apply to math and science as well as social studies, for example)?

Begin with the idea that the theme is a lens that reveals the connections within the world. Now, consider the following themes. Which are better:

- *patterns or bears*
- *change or dinosaurs*
- *World War I or cycles*

Did you choose: patterns, change, and cycles. Regie Routman (1991) has this to say about thematic units:

> Unfortunately, many of the thematic units teachers buy and create are nothing more than suggested activities clustered around a central focus or topic. These units incorporate some elements of math, science, social studies, art, and music, but there is often little or no development of important ideas. This is correlation, not integration. With integration, the relationships among the disciplines or subject areas are meaningful and natural. Concepts identified are not only related to the topic or subject but are important to them. With correlation the connections are superficial and forced, and there is no important concept development.
>
> Superficial units or themes that focus on such topics as the circus, cars, bears, animals, monsters, dragons, mice, pigs, and kites, are commonly used in the elementary grades and are good examples of correlations... I believe that we need to be investing most of our time in conscious, deliberate, thoughtful topics and themes that go beyond the literal level (p. 277).

Some school districts have established themes by grade level to assist teachers in avoiding the pitfalls of selecting irrelevant or cutesy themes. For example, the South Central School District, Washington, established the following themes to help students find the interconnectedness of their studies:

Kindergarten–Explorations
Grade 1–Relationships
Grade 2–Community
Grade 3–Connections
Grade 4–Cultures
Grade 5–Conflict and Change

Grade 6–Perspectives
Grade 7–Origins
Grade 8–Identity
Grade 9–Discovery
Grade 10–Culture, Change and Conflict
Grade 11–Individual and Society
Grade 12–Vistas, Visions and Futures

BEGIN BY WORKING BACKWARDS

When you plan your first thematic unit, begin by working backwards. What did you teach last year? Brainstorm all the topics and chapters—even chapter titles—that you taught, by subject, and perhaps even by month. Spread them out on a large sheet of chart paper and look for connections. Are there some meaningful and natural relationships that connect these various topics? Do they share a common theme? For example, in social studies last year you had a unit on social skills and a unit on citizenship. In science you had a unit on the seasons and a unit on weather. In health you had a unit on nutrition. In language arts you studied families and friends. Looking across all of these topics, you'll notice that the common theme of relationships is pervasive and natural. Relationships would be an appropriate theme. It cuts across all of the disciplines and yet it permeates each individual discipline. It's the glue that holds together topics taught previously in an isolated, fragmented fashion.

LENGTH OF TIME

What period of time does a theme cover? The answer can range anywhere from a one-day integrated unit to a thematic unit that lasts a week to several weeks, or a theme that covers the entire school year. If you're new to thematic planning, a one- or two-week program of activities will be much easier to plan and implement than a theme designed for a year.

WEBBING THE CONNECTIONS

The second step in developing a thematic unit is to brainstorm the associations or the connections. An easy way to begin is to use a mind map or a web as a graphic organizer, using your theme as the organizing center. The spokes of your web can be the disciplines you teach. Remember, when brainstorming you want a quantity of ideas; you're not concerned about quality right now. Look for as many connections possible.

The following webs were developed by elementary teachers. They brainstormed connections to integrate their various disciplines with a common theme or an organizing center.

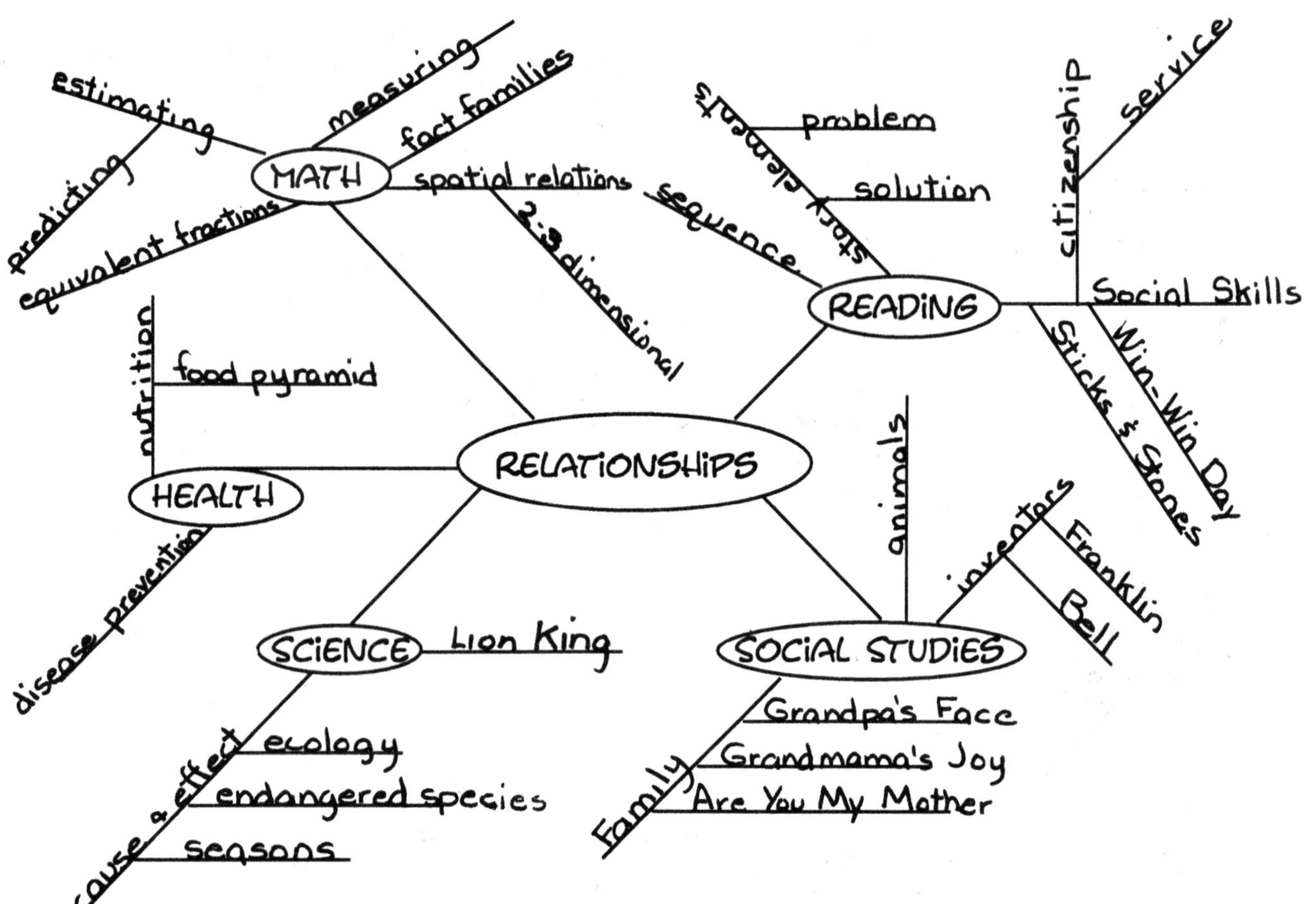

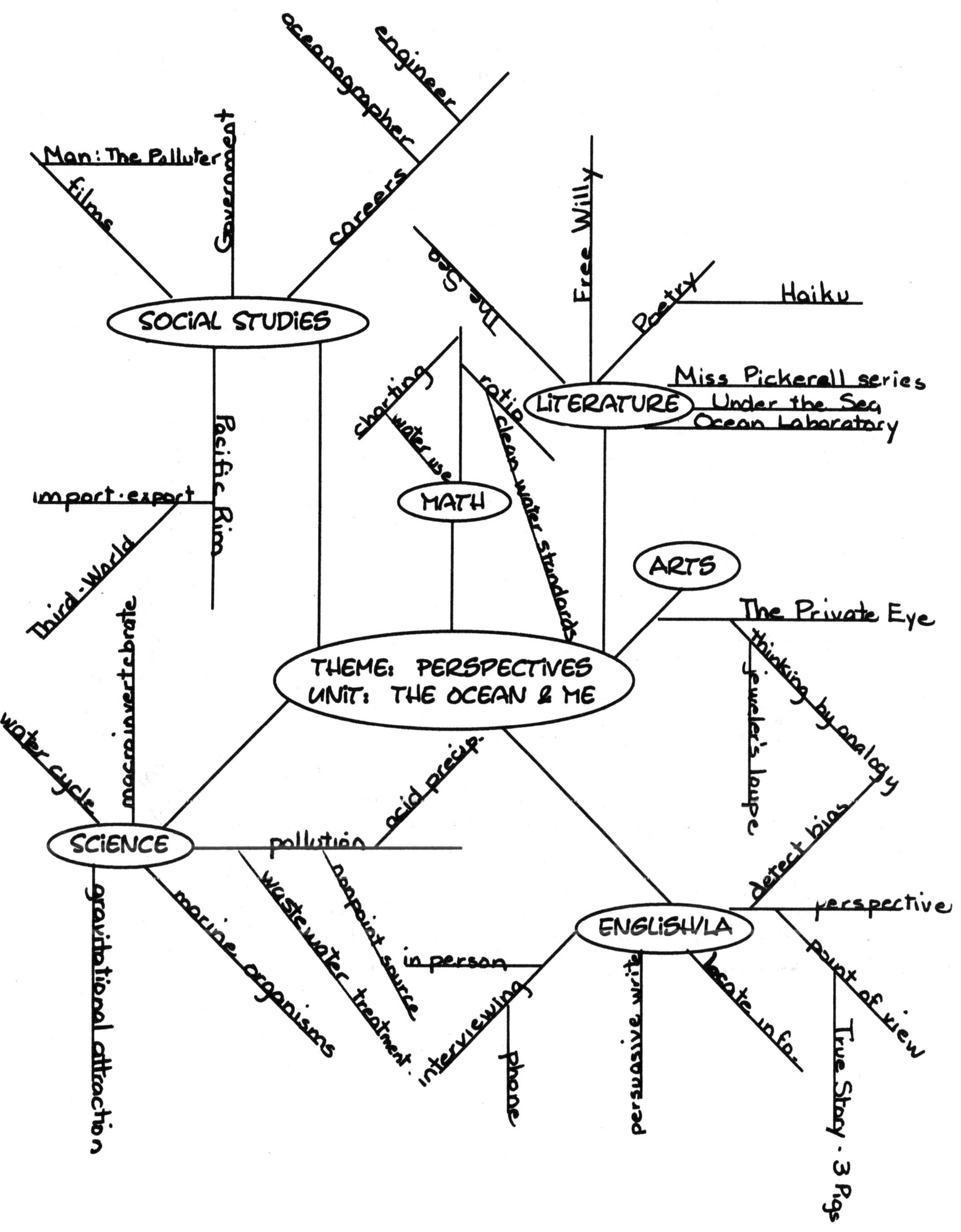
THEME: PERSPECTIVES
UNIT: THE OCEAN & ME
SOCIAL STUDIES
Man: The Polluter
films
Government
careers
oceanographer
engineer
Pacific Rim
import · export
Third-World
LITERATURE
The Sea
Free Willy
Poetry
Haiku
Miss Pickerell series
Under the Sea
Ocean Laboratory
MATH
charting
water use
ratio
clean water standards
ARTS
The Private Eye
jeweler's loupe
thinking by analogy
SCIENCE
water cycle
macroinvertebrate
pollution
acid precip.
nonpoint source
wastewater treatment
marine organisms
gravitational attraction
ENGLISH/LA
detect bias
perspective
point of view
True Story · 3 Pigs
locate info.
persuasive write
interviewing
in person
phone

GUIDING QUESTIONS

A good theme cuts across disciplines. In your web you identified connections to the theme by discipline, which shows that the theme relates to each one. However, the disciplines remain unconnected. Your next step is to look for organizers (guiding questions) that will link the disciplines (Jacobs, 1989). The number of connections you found to your organizing center (theme) may number in the hundreds. Now try to find a few broad, organizing topics that can be addressed by more than one discipline and write them as questions. These guiding questions will help you design authentic activities for the unit. (Don't forget to post your web and your guiding questions for students to study. They may want to add connections and questions themselves.)

RELATIONSHIPS

1. HOW DO I RELATE TO
   - MY FAMILY?
   - MY SCHOOL?
   - MY NEIGHBORHOOD?
   - MY WORLD?
2. HOW DO RELATIONSHIPS CHANGE?
3. WHAT RELATIONSHIPS ARE INTERDEPENDENT?
4. WHERE ARE CAUSE-EFFECT RELATIONSHIPS FOUND IN NATURE?
5. HOW DO WE MEASURE CAUSE-EFFECT RELATIONSHIPS?
6. WHAT CONTROL DO I HAVE OVER CAUSE-EFFECT RELATIONSHIPS?

PERSPECTIVES: THE OCEAN & ME

1. WHO IS DEPENDENT ON THE OCEAN?
2. WHAT IS THE OCEAN DEPENDENT UPON?
3. HOW HAS THE OCEAN CHANGED?
3. WHAT'S BEST FOR THE FUTURE OF THE OCEAN FROM THE PERSPECTIVE OF
   - SEA LIFE/ANIMALS
   - BUSINESS/INDUSTRY
   - MYSELF

ALIGNMENT

Before planning the activities for your unit of study, take a look at your district standards, benchmarks, or objectives. They will (1) become the filter through which you analyze which connections on your web to keep with your guiding questions, and (2) help you develop the authentic tasks and activities for your unit.

CONTENT STANDARDS

The activities and tasks selected for students in a unit need to be aligned with and directed toward the district performance standards. In the following table, look first at the third column examples of performance objectives found in elementary grades. Then study the first column, connections to the theme from the web for *relationships*. What activities or tasks can you think of that tie the thematic connection both to the guiding question and to district performance standards?

Thematic Connections from *relationships*	**Tasks/activities**	**Content/skills (performance standards)**
ENDANGERED SPECIES	?	counting
FOOD CHAIN		graphing
FACT FAMILIES	?	sort into categories
FAMILIES		recognize patterns
SOCIAL SKILLS	?	summarize
NUTRITION		draw conclusions
CAUSE/EFFECT	?	recognize elements of fiction
CITIZENSHIP		write a friendly letter
	?	record & report on observations

COMPLEX THINKING STANDARDS

What level of thinking will be required from the students when demonstrating the content? What are the expectations for complex thinking and reasoning skills? For example, students may be asked to compare, to classify, to make inductions and deductions, to abstract, to investigate, to invent, to problem-solve, and to make appropriate decisions. Just knowing your district expectations for content standards is not enough—you must also know the standards for complexity of thinking.

COMMUNICATION STANDARDS

In addition to complex thinking standards, under what conditions will students be expected to perform? Many districts have established performance-based objectives for communication skills that cut across all of the disciplines. Communication standards include working cooperatively, making both oral and visual presentations, listening and responding, setting relevant goals, and evaluating both oral and visual presentations.

Planning the Task

CONTENT STANDARDS	COMPLEX THINKING	COMMUNICATION STANDARDS
Declarative information	Compare	Cooperation
Procedural information	Classify	Information processing
Generalizations	Induct/deduct	Metacognition
	Abstract	High-quality products
	Invent	Oral & visual presentations
	Investigate	Listening/responding
	Problem solve	Goal setting
	Decision making	

DESIGNING <u>AUTHENTIC</u> TASKS FOR STUDENTS

So far, we have (1) selected a theme to use as an organizing center; (2) made connections across all of the disciplines; (3) developed guiding questions; and (4) taken a look at district performance standards to guide in the last step, the selection of authentic tasks for students.

District performance standards typically include both complex thinking skills and content knowledge that students must be able to perform or accomplish. What makes these standards *authentic*, however, is another dimension. Newman and Wehlage (1993) developed the guide below to judge the *authenticity* of student tasks. Ask yourself the following questions:

1. Am I asking the student to do something significant, or is it something trivial?
2. Does the task require higher order thinking or is it rote regurgitation of information?
3. Is the knowledge deep or is it rather superficial and shallow?
4. Is this activity connected to the outside world? Is it something students will do in the real world or is there no connection whatsoever?
5. Does this task require substantive conversation or is it performed alone, with no interaction?

Let's answer each of the above questions using the concept of interdependence from the relationships unit. One of the brainstormed associations was with the Disney musical, *The Lion King.* Authentic tasks for students might include:

- Describe and create a visual aid to show the interdependent relationships in the story.
- Write a poem or a short story that demonstrates what would happen if everyone had the problem-free philosophy described in *Hakuna Matata.*

1. Studying the interdependence of our ecosystem and looking at our role in preserving this precious system are both *significant* tasks (in contrast to coloring pictures from the story).

2. Both tasks require higher-level thinking, including analysis and prediction.

3. Students will need a deep understanding of several significant concepts (e.g., food chain, endangered species, interdependence, ecosystem) in order to complete the tasks.

4. These tasks also address real-world problems (as compared to activities that are found only in schools and not beyond).

5. When the performance standard for these two tasks requires small group consensus, substantive conversation follows.

When designing an *authentic* task, then, consider both the five questions developed by Newman and Wehlage and the assessment standards developed by your school district (content standards, complex thinking standards, and communication standards). Here's what your thought process might sound like as you develop an *authentic* task for the unit, *Perspectives on the Ocean*:

"I need to consider content standards, reasoning and complex thinking skills, as well as how the task is to be demonstrated. Content standards could include information related to the water cycle, food chain, and animal habitats. Complex thinking skills might require investigation and prediction. Students could be challenged with questions like: How do I relate to the ocean, as a student? How does a fisherman relate to the ocean? How do members of Greenpeace relate to the ocean? One meaningful task might be to ask students to identify and investigate one person or group with direct contact or a close relationship to the ocean; obtain an interview, conduct the interview; communicate their findings and conclusions to the class either visually or orally. This task will require considerable interaction and dialogue. It will require students to get involved with the community as well as to do some personal problem solving as they take a position on an issue."

CRAP DETECTION

Hemingway once said, "To be a good writer one must have a built-in, shock-proof, crap detector." To develop quality activities for a thematic unit, a teacher needs to have a built-in, shock-proof *crap detector*. Too often teachers try to force a fit in designing activities for a thematic unit. For example, in our thematic unit on relationships, your *crap detector* should flicker if you see a teacher provide a child with a worksheet that has a word search in which the student is expected to find the word "relationship." Or, if students are asked to take the word "relationship" and see how many small words they can make from that larger word. This is not only forcing a fit, but when we look at our district standards and our lifelong learning goals, these two activities do not help accomplish any performance standard. Brophy and Alleman (1991) issue the following cautions:

- "Just because an activity crosses subject-matter lines does not make it worthwhile; it must also help accomplish important educational goals."

- "Many of these activities...
  -are pointless busywork (alphabetizing the state capitals)
  -require time-consuming artistic or construction work
  -sometimes even distort social studies content
  -require students to do things that are strange, difficult, or even impossible
  -call for students to do things they are not prepared to do either because the task is ambiguous (drawing a hungry face) or because it requires them to use knowledge that has not been taught in the curriculum..." (p. 66)

Use performance standards as a filter to guide the development of activities for a thematic unit. For example, one of the connections in *relationships* is the study of nutrition. One performance standard is to compare and contrast. An authentic activity might be to have students compare and contrast the new food pyramid with the foods they ate the previous day.

To foster the complex thinking skill of decision-making, students might be asked to decide whether or not they were eating well-balanced meals. To develop the complex thinking skill of problem-solving, students might develop a plan to help them eat better-balanced meals. Communication standards are built into the task by giving students the option of how they will present their information to the class.

PRACTICE ACTIVITY: THE OCEAN AND ME

The following examples are for you to practice discriminating which tasks would both be authentic and help accomplish performance standards, and which ones are not a good use of student time.

1. Whom would you contact (a) to find out when fishing season opens; (b) to report an oil spill; (c) if you're concerned about the dumping of waste? Explain your answers.

2. Unscramble this word: deeitnsm

3. Select one marine organism. Draw a graphic to place it in the food web. Explain the effect on this organism of an oil spill.

4. Find three news articles in a recent newspaper that have implications for the future of the ocean. Explain the implications.

5. Use your dictionary to define the following terms: plankton, technology, biodegradable.

Hopefully, you checked tasks 1, 3, and 4 as being most authentic. Five would be more authentic if students had to re-write the dictionary definition in their own words, requiring them to think, instead of simply copying a definition out of the dictionary. It's important to keep performance standards in front of us and use them as a filter in developing activities for a thematic unit.

AVOIDING TRIVIAL PURSUIT

"If a man does not know to which port he is sailing, no wind is favorable." Seneca may have said this back in the first century A.D., but it's also true today. To avoid developing trivial activities from a thematic unit, tasks should be planned only alongside content standards. Only then will congruence and alignment be achieved. The beauty of designing tasks requiring depth of understanding and authentic communication is that the task becomes the *performance used for assessment!* Now, through "kid watching," portfolios, self-assessments, and projects, assessment and performance tasks may become one!

Wiggins (1995) calls this *"Backwards Design"*. He argues that a performance task should "...count as compelling and valid evidence that students have understood what is to be learned..." (p. 104). This is an ongoing assessment of their successive approximations of learning. No longer do we work from the bottom up, the old scope and sequence paradigm (e.g., teach 200 discrete skills and give a mastery test). Districts often establish benchmarks—standards against which performances may be measured—to help profile a student's achievement. (More on this is in Chapter Seven.)

CURRICULUM MAP

The curriculum map is an additional tool to facilitate planning. It adds the dimension of time to a thematic unit (see p. 28). The unit theme and connections across the disciplines are given a time framework (the school year). This is particularly important if you have specific units of study for which you are accountable; make sure you are accomplishing content coverage as well as looking at thematic planning from a broader perspective, or a broader lens.

Always keep in mind that not all subjects and topics will fit into your theme. Indeed, some are taught better within the discipline, not across disciplines. Kathleen Roth (1994), in *Second Thoughts About Interdisciplinary Studies,* reminds us that some science concepts are better taught in isolation, not in an integrated fashion. For example, she wanted to teach her students about the biology of plants and needed the time to do that without having to compromise or dilute this needed instruction in order to fit a broader theme. She ends her article with the following caveat, "Before we jump on the interdisciplinary bandwagon, let us engage in debate and study of the kinds of integration that are compelling, meaningful, and powerful for children."

Use Roth's caveat as you take one last look at the curriculum map that you do for the year. Make sure that you're not forcing a fit. Identify which units or topics will be taught *within* the discipline and which ones will fit naturally across your disciplines.

The curriculum map may also be used at the beginning of planning a thematic unit. Begin by listing all the units/topics/lessons you would normally teach, by month and by discipline. Then look for natural connections. If you see a common thread/concept across several of your units, re-sequence the teaching of these related topics under the umbrella theme (as described earlier in this chapter).

SUMMARY

A thematic unit becomes the planning guide for activities in a diverse classroom. Reading and writing activities, learning centers, and assessment may be connected through the theme. Students are helped to see the big picture, the *cover of the jigsaw puzzle,* which helps them avoid getting lost among isolated bits and pieces of information. By planning backwards, with a major concept/theme in mind, teachers are less likely to insert trivial or unrelated content into an already crowded curriculum.

Curriculum Map for

Theme ▼		Reading	Language	Social Studies	Math	Science	Thinking Skills	Social Skills	Service
Sept.									
Oct.									
Nov.									
Dec.									
Jan.									
Feb.									
Mar.									
Apr.									
May									
June									

CHAPTER 3

READING TO READ

Consider the following four weekend activities. If you were to rank order them in terms of preference, what would you do first, second, third, and fourth? Here are your choices:

1. You could spend the day outdoors.
2. Or your might prefer to spend your time at the computer, playing computer games.
3. Perhaps you'd like to enjoy a few television programs.
4. Finally, you might curl up with a book and read.

Now, switch roles. You are now a typical student. What would you pick first, second, third, and fourth? You may have picked reading or being outdoors as first or second choice. And yet when you had to change roles and predict what your students would pick first and second, did you pick computer games or watching television?

Indeed, children today are spending over 30 hours a week in front of the television—almost the equivalent of a full-time job. What does that mean for us today as teachers? What it means is that we have our work cut out for us. If students aren't going to pick reading as their first choice, if there are many other things that they'd rather be doing than reading, we have a tremendous job ahead of us. We must motivate students to want to read.

Why is it important to motivate students to want to read? Success in reading is essential for success in school. As early as the third grade, we can predict who our at-risk learners are—who are in danger of not completing school with an adequate level of skills—by identifying those who are not reading at grade level (Slavin & Madden, 1989). We can get our students reading at grade level by the third grade and therefore reduce this risk factor. We can motivate students to want to read, both for pleasure and for gathering information. How? That's what this chapter is all about!

The chapter will be divided into the four components of a balanced reading program. The components are listed on the following chart:

READING TO STUDENTS	GUIDED READING
Expert model Motivate with enthusiasm Audio tapes	Activating background information Story structures & strategies Grapho-phonics cues
SHARED READING-REPEATED READING	**READING ALONE**
Signature reading Pairing/sharing Train reading Ear to hear/partner reading Break-in Popcorn reading Hot potato Echo reading Do you want to hear me read? (anthology)	DEAR, NIB, KBAR, USSR Reading Tubs Homework: • Monthly calendar • Weekly assignment sheet • Homework coupons

READING TO STUDENTS

Take the following true/false quiz adapted from *The Reading Teacher.*

Reading to students:

1. Helps them do better in beginning reading. T or F
2. Increases their abilities to read on their own. T or F
3. Improves listening skill. T or F
4. Increases their vocabularies. T or F
5. Improves reading comprehension. T or F
6. Helps them speak better. T or F
7. Helps them become better writers. T or F
8. Improves the quality and amount of what students write on their own. T or F

If you answered true to all of the items on the quiz, you're right!

Did you know that the single most important thing you can do to motivate kids to read—to get them ready to read—is to read aloud to them? Hearing the expert read aloud improves listening comprehension, which is necessary for reading comprehension.

ENTHUSIASM

Show enthusiasm while reading:

- Vary your voice level.
- Use animated facial expressions.
- Use hand and large body movements to illustrate ideas.
- Encourage your listeners to participate as you read along.
- Provide positive support for their participation.
- Model vitality and a high energy level.

As you read aloud to students, let your voice take on the roles of the characters. You're providing the model of the script that students will replay in their own minds when they eventually read the same story alone.

AUDIO TAPES

When you don't have time to read aloud to students, put the stories on audio tapes. At a listening center, let them enjoy following the story along in a book or just listening. Or, let the whole class listen to the cassette while you monitor and help them track in their copy of the story.

GUIDED READING

Guided reading is the instructional part of your reading program. The definition of reading is fairly simple: making sense out of squiggly marks on a page. How can we help students make sense out of squiggly marks on a page?

Let's try an experiment. I'm going to give you a sentence with a word missing. You fill in the missing word. "He _______ away." What did you pick for the missing word? By any chance did you pick a verb? Did you pick a past tense verb? If you did, you were making sense from the basic structure of the two words that were already there. When we try to make sense using the structure and patterns of language, we're using *syntactic cues*.

Now, if you read on, the next sentence in this passage says, "The barn was on fire." Now go back and look at the word you picked. You know that because there's a fire, you're going to use your past experience (knowledge of the subject), *semantic knowledge*, and will make sure the word fits with what you know about a fire. You're likely to run away from a fire, so you may select *ran*, instead of *walked*.

Continue to read the passage: "The barn was on fire. He g________ away. Fire frightens horses." Now knowing that horses are frightened of fire, the barn is on fire, and the missing word starts with a 'g', you're likely to substitute the word "galloped." You used three cueing systems to make sense out of a word that you didn't know.

Cueing Systems

1. The structure and pattern of language (*syntactic knowledge*)
2. Your past experience or knowledge of the subject (*semantic knowledge*)
3. Your knowledge of word beginnings & endings, clusters or patterns of letters, prefixes, suffixes (*grapho-phonic knowledge*)

A guided reading system utilizes all three of these cueing systems to help learners make sense out of squiggly marks on a page. What follows are strategies to consider for guided reading: activating background information, teaching story structure, and teaching grapho-phonic strategies.

ACTIVATING BACKGROUND INFORMATION

The first strategy of a guided reading lesson occurs before our students even open the book they are reading. Help them make use of *semantic information*: bringing their past experiences to the printed page. The following activities can be used to activate background information: KWL, Double Bubble, Word Splash, Word Sort, Round Table, and Picture Reading.

KWL

K (What You <u>K</u>now)	W (What You <u>W</u>ant To Know)	L (What You <u>L</u>earned)
1.	1.	1.
2.	2.	2.
3.	3.	3.

The K and the W columns will be filled in first. For instance, if you're about to read a story about plants, have students brainstorm in small cooperative groups what they already know about plants. Then ask them to generate questions. What don't you know about plants? At the end of the story, let them go back and fill in what they learned (L column). For any questions not answered, add a column: "How can we find out?"

DOUBLE BUBBLE

Use Double Bubble when you're beginning a story (or subject) that's similar to one students read before. For example, during a unit on social skills, the students finished the book, *Sticks and Stones*. Hold up the book *Sticks and Stones*, with the new book the students are about to read, *Copy the Cat*. Show the covers to the class, asking: "How are these two books the same?" Students might notice right away they're by the same author. Or, they might notice that they're both about making friends. Or, they both have animals as main characters. After reading the new story, complete the Double Bubble with more likenesses and differences.

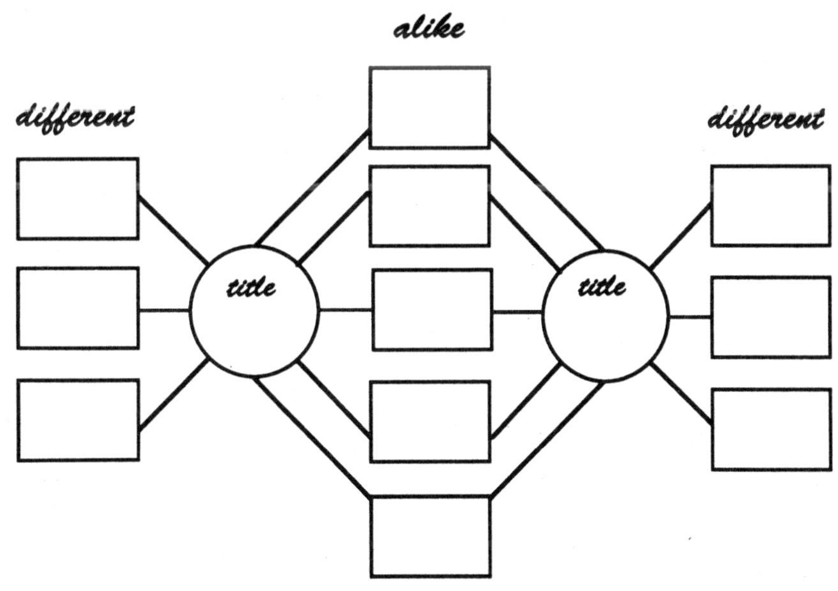

WORD SPLASH

To create a word splash, identify vocabulary words that are related to the topic of the story. For example, if the topic is about being angry, put *angry* in the center of a chart. Scatter the vocabulary words around *angry*. Ask students to make a connection by using each vocabulary word in a sentence with the word *angry*. For example, students might generate sentences like "Some problems make me angry."

WORD SORT

A Word Sort helps learners categorize concepts or ideas from the story. For instance if you're reading about explorers, scramble a list of vocabulary words that the students will encounter in their reading. The word sort is even more fun if the words are placed on word cards, one set per cooperative group, and students get to rearrange them. Ask students to group the words. They get to pick the categories.

Columbus Champlain Cabot

Portugal Magellan France

Incas Marco Polo Pizarro

Cortez Aztec Indians Spain Ponce de Leon

ROUND TABLE

In Round Table, each cooperative group passes a sheet of paper around the group to which they add an idea related to the topic of the story they are about to read. Let's say you're reading a mystery. Introduce the new story by saying, "We know a lot about mysteries already. If you know you're about to read another mystery, what predictions might you make? Pass your sheet of paper, each person add one word and tell your group why."

For example, one student might say, "I wrote *detective* because a detective is usually a main character." Students end up with a potential list of vocabulary words and cognitive connections to the story they're about to read.

PICTURE READING

Perhaps one of the easiest ways to activate background knowledge is to ask students to interpret the pictures in a book before they actually read the text. Simply ask them, "What do you already know about the book from just looking at the illustration on the cover? Go through and look only at the pictures and see if you can predict what the story is going to be about." Unfortunately, poor readers seldom look at the pictures. They pick up a book and begin reading on the first page of the story, reading the text and pronouncing the words. If they learned to look at the pictures first, they would be activating much more meaning and bringing that meaning to the printed page.

Another simple strategy to help students make predictions is to see if they could predict what the story was going to be about just from looking at the cover of the book. Ask them to either tell their study buddy or to write on their Think Pad, what their predictions are. Have them stop in the middle of the story and confirm whether their predictions were accurate or not. Did they identify the problem? the characters? Then, either with their study buddy or on their Think Pad, predict the solution to the story. Let them finish reading the story and check the accuracy of their solution prediction.

Any of the strategies thus far described will help students by helping them dig into their past experiences. Being alerted to these past experiences, they're more likely to comprehend the story that you're about to begin. In the old, traditional word card method, the teacher would hold up a card and say, "This word is 'principal.' What does it say, class? Say it with me." Mimicry does not activate background knowledge, nor does a student learn to read a word by simply seeing a flashcard.

STORY STRUCTURES/STORY GRAMMAR

A second strategy of the guided reading lesson is to help your students make use of *syntactical knowledge*: making sense out of reading by looking at relationships and patterns within both expository and narrative writing. Good literature has predictable text structure.

STORY CHARTS

In narrative writing, story structure helps develop student comprehension. A well-written story has a setting and characters, a problem and solution. The next few pages include charts to help students recognize story structure or "story grammar." Students can choose one of these approaches:

- Fill in a story structure chart as they read.
- Stop at strategic places in the story, discuss it with their study buddy, or even make a prediction about the solution.
- Fill in a story structure chart when they are finished reading the story.

STORY STRUCTURE CHARTS

To help students see that good literature has a predictable pattern, keep a class chart or let students keep a personal record of the story elements for a particular book series. For a unit on fairy tales, your chart might look like this:

Story Structure: Fairy Tales

Title	Characters	Setting	Problem	Solution
Goldilocks & The Three Bears				
Cinderella				
The Three Billy Goats Gruff				
The Little Red Hen				

As a cooperative group activity, draw the following chart on a large mural. Assign each cooperative group one element to illustrate and describe, or have each member of a group develop a different box. Students could also work independently on this story grammar.

Main Character (Who?)	**Setting (Where?)**
Problem (What's wrong?)	**Event #1 (What happened?)**
Event #2 (What happened next?)	**Solution (How was the problem solved?)**

What I liked best about this story:

Sentence starters or prompts will also help students make sense out of what they're reading.

Title

The problem in this story was

This was a problem because

The problem was finally solved when

In the end,

The sequence of a story can be developed with the following chart.

Problem	Action	Results

To highlight story sequence, this chart can be filled in as the children read, or afterwards. Concepts such as beginning and end of story are developed. Tailor the chart to fit the number of major events in the story.

In the beginning,	
Event #1	
Event #2	
Event #3	
Event #4	
Finally,	

CHAPTER BOOKS

Help students see patterns and follow story sequence when they're in chapter books. Before they read the next chapter, ask students to go back and summarize the one they just read. As they read each chapter, have students identify two main or central ideas and give the details for each. Because chapter books don't have many illustrations, students may draw pictures, cartoons, or diagrams to go with each central idea. This could be organized as a response log, with a separate page for each chapter, adding space for students to write their own reactions to the chapter.

<table>
<tr><td>Review:
Chapter __ was about</td><td></td></tr>
<tr><td>New:
Chapter __

(illustrate)</td><td>Main idea #1:

Detail:

Detail:</td></tr>
<tr><td>(illustrate)</td><td>Main idea #2:

Detail:

Detail:</td></tr>
<tr><td>My response

I like/dislike....
I wish....
I felt....
I predict....
I question....
It reminds me....
I would change....</td><td></td></tr>
</table>

Title: Author:

A strategic reader will summarize *while* reading, making sense out of what he has read so far. In addition, a strategic reader will continue to ask himself questions about the story *as* he reads. Perhaps in the middle of the story he'll make a prediction as to how the story is going to end. Design story structure charts that encourage these behaviors.

SUMMARIZATION

Another easy strategy to use for expository text is to combine the problem-solution strategy with summarization. Give students a pattern to fill in, such as "________ had a problem because _____________. Therefore, ______. As a result, ________." Asking students to summarize in this way periodically throughout a chapter or story has been found to improve their comprehension.

Most of the strategies described so far will work for both narrative and expository writing. For instance, problem-solution structure can be found very often in history textbooks. What was the problem? Why did they move westward? Why did the pilgrims come to the new country? What was the solution?

MULTI-PASS

One technique specific to expository (non-fiction) writing is called *multi-pass*. Teach students to use format clues in textural writing to help them organize the chapter information. Scanning headings, sub-headings, chapter summaries, and chapter questions first will improve comprehension. The strategy is called *multi-pass* because readers pass through the chapter several times. One pass through is to read the **boldface** or *italics*, another is to read headings and sub-headings; another is to study the illustrations. When first teaching this strategy, have students check which strategies they used when they passed through the chapter.

Multi-Pass for Chapters

	1	2	3	4
Headings				
Subheadings				
Bold print				
Italics				
Chapter summary				
Pictures				
Graphics				
Objectives				
Chapter questions				
Vocabulary list				

Use multi-pass as a warm-up activity. If you are about to begin a new chapter, your warm-up might sound like one of the following:

- Scan Chapter 7 for terms in **bold print** or *italics*. Make 2 lists, terms you know and terms you don't know.

- Read the chapter summary. Write two possible test questions for the chapter.

- Find one illustration in Chapter 7. Brainstorm a written list of everything you can learn from only studying the illustration.

- Read the questions at the end of Chapter 7. Write down three main points you will look for as you read the chapter.

GRAPHO-PHONICS CUES

From the earlier experiment you found that comprehension, or making meaning, is based upon three cueing systems: semantic clues, that is, your past experiences; syntactic cues, knowing and understanding the patterns; and grapho-phonic cues. Yes, even in the whole language classroom, phonics need to be taught.

LETTER KNOWLEDGE

What do beginning readers need to know? "Prereaders' letter knowledge was the single best predictor of first-year reading achievement, with their ability to discriminate phonemes auditorily ranking a close second" (Adams, 1990, p. 36). Because so many of our at-risk learners enter school without letter knowledge or letter-sound awareness, the explicit teaching of both is recommended. The goal is to increase the speed with which letters and other phonemes are recognized. The resulting automaticity allows for fluent reading and activation of the other cueing systems.

Teaching phonics in context is much more fun and makes much more sense than teaching it in isolation. For example, if you're reading "big books" with a rhyming pattern, the predictability of the rhyme will help learners see phonetic patterns.

Regie Routman (1991) suggests a teaching *order* for phonics:

- Beginning consonants
- Ending consonants
- Consonant digraphs
- Medial consonants
- Consonant blends
- Long vowels
- Short vowels

SYLLABLES

Fluent readers are able to break long words into syllables. Because of the unreliability of phonic generalizations, it has been found more useful to teach rhyming word families. These "syllable families" are predictable for both spoken and written language. The following 37 "rhyming families" are found in 500 primary-grade words (Adams, 1990).

-ack	-all	-ain	-ake	-ale	-ame	-an
-ank	-ap	-ash	-at	-ate	-aw	-ay
-eat	-ell	-est	-ice	-ick	-ide	-ight
-ill	-in	-ine	-ing	-ink	-ip	-ir
-ock	-oke	-op	-or	-ore	-uck	-ug
-ump	-unk					

Make a chart of these rhyming families. For young children, put the rhyming words in the same box.

-at			*-an*			*-ip*			*-op*		
rat	pat	sat	man	Nan	fan	sip	ship	zip	pop	shop	mop
flat	chat	that	van	can	tan	dip	rip	drip	crop	chop	cop
fat	mat	brat	ban	ran	pan	nip	chip	lip	flop	hop	top
bat	scat	hat	clan	Stan	than	whip	hip	tip	stop		

Primary and intermediate children love riddles. Hink Pink (or, Hinky Pinky for 2 syllables or Hinkety Pinkety for three syllables) provides practice in reading the rhyming families as well as in vocabulary development. For example, the teacher might begin by saying: "Hink Pink: ant's carpet." The answer must be two one-syllable words from the same family: bug rug. When students are just learning to play the game, lower the level of difficulty by telling them in which family (i.e., ug) the answer can be found. Eventually, students begin making up their own riddles. These riddles are fun warm-up or sponge activities. Here are a few to get started:

soft drink deli (op family--*pop shop*)
award-winning policeman (op family--*top cop*)
cream-colored vehicle (an family--*tan van*)
ruined vegetable garden (op family--*crop flop*)

In addition, there are many natural strategies to use in the classroom, such as asking students to keep their own personal phonics booklets; doing phonics charts on the wall; having lots of shared reading opportunities; reading poetry with rhyme, using the *cloze* procedure to let the kids fill in a rhyming word and then look at the word with which it rhymes. It might sound like this:

Cloze Procedure

What will the day bring? The choice is mine.
It could be bad. It could be _________.
What word should we put in the blank?
Watch me write it: *fine.* Now look at how "mine" is spelled. Do you see a pattern?

DIAGNOSING GRAPHO-PHONIC SKILLS

Phonics canNOT be left out of the teaching of reading. In fact, phonological awareness is the best predictor of *reading progress* in young children (Stanovich, 1994). Stanovich has found that the following phonological awareness tasks are better predictors of reading success than an IQ test. You can use this list as a diagnostic tool to identify a child's grapho-phonic needs.

- Phoneme deletion (Take away the initial consonant in sit, what word is left?)
- Word to word matching (Do these words begin with the same sound: *bat* and *bike*?)
- Blending (What word do these sounds make: /c/ /a/ /t/?)

- Sound isolation (What sound is at the beginning of *pen*?)
- Phoneme counting (Count the sounds in the word *bike*.)
- Deleted phoneme (What sound is in *fall* but missing from the word *all*?)
- Odd word out (Which word begins with a different sound: *mat, mitt, fall, mike*?)
- Sound-to-word matching (Is there a /p/ sound in the word *cap*?)

Children who have not been exposed to print won't necessarily discover grapho-phonic principles on their own. Stanovich, citing numerous researchers, concludes that "...direct instruction in alphabetic coding facilitates early reading acquisition...." (1994, p. 286).

READING GROUPS

Research is very convincing that the practice of "bluebird and buzzard" reading groups is no longer appropriate. Permanent, homogeneous grouping labels students and becomes a self-propelling prophecy: once a buzzard always a buzzard. It's very difficult to get out of that particular group.

HETEROGENEOUS AND FLEXIBLE GROUPING

Today, we're looking at heterogeneous groupings, as well as homogeneous, *flexible* skill groupings. There should be many different ways to group students during the communication arts period. For example, you may use one core book to develop your thematic unit with your whole class, using guided reading strategies. At the same time you have small skills groups based on specific needs. During independent reading time students may be reading self-selected books. Or, small groups may be formed based on student interest in reading a particular book. You are the ultimate designer in a whole language classroom!

The Joplin Plan groups students homogeneously by class during guided reading time only. For example, students change rooms during the reading block only. This homogeneous grouping, placing low-level readers together in one room or high-level readers in another, is easier for whole group guided instruction. What will make this most effective, however, and not just a translation of the buzzard, bluebird, and eagle reading groups from the old days, is that these groups must remain flexible. When a student's reading level changes, he is immediately placed in the appropriate group. And, perhaps even more important, students continue to get a balanced, heterogeneous reading program in their regular classroom. When students return to their regular classroom they should have opportunity for repeated readings, expert readings, and reading alone. Even the Joplin Plan should not eliminate selected thematic books for whole class instruction of integrated units.

A WHOLE GROUP READING LESSON

To encourage strategic reading and the use of cueing systems in a lesson with multiple ability levels, the following cooperative learning strategies increase success for all:

ROUND TABLE to activate background information
THREE-STEP INTERVIEW to use story structure, make a prediction
NUMBERED HEADS to increase story comprehension

ROUND TABLE

Students work in groups of three or four and brainstorm what they already know about a given topic on a sheet or paper (or transparency, using overhead projector pens). If the class is about to read another mystery, the teacher says, "Brainstorm everything you know about mystery stories." Each team member writes one idea or mystery-related word down and passes the paper to the next team member.

When groups share their ideas, the structure of the mystery story is reviewed (i.e., characters = criminal, detective; problem = crime), and vocabulary words are introduced. To provide for multiple readings and expert reading of the text, the teacher might begin reading aloud to students. Students then read silently to the middle of the story where the problem is clearly established, but the solution is not. Strategic readers both summarize frequently during reading and make predictions. When students know that they will routinely be stopping in the middle of a story to predict the solution, they're more likely to be identifying important information or clues to the solution as they read the first half. Now it's time for the next cooperative activity to promote strategic reading.

THREE-STEP INTERVIEW

This was designed for groups of four but can be adapted to partnerships. For a three-step interview, students:

1. Form pairs and interview their partners: "What do you think the problem is? What do you predict the solution will be?"

2. Reverse the interview, asking the same questions.
3. If teams have four members, pairs now form into groups of four and go around the group sharing what their partners predicted in the interview.

The students then finish reading the story. Motivation is high when students continue reading to find out if their predictions were correct!

NUMBERED HEADS

Instead of using the typical worksheet filled with story comprehension questions, students work together to answer questions dictated by the teacher. Writing them on the overhead projector makes it easier for students to refer to them when consulting with peers.

1. Students are numbered in each team: 1, 2, 3, 4.
2. Teacher gives one question (e.g., "What clues did the detective use?") and says, "Heads together." Students confer in their teams, agreeing upon an answer.
3. Teacher says, "Heads up, one's up." The number called should be randomly selected. Throw a Styrofoam die or use a spinner.
4. In each team, the person with the number called stands. If the answer is one or two words, you can ask for a choral response from all members standing. If you call on one person at the time, the speaker begins the answer with the words, "My team says...."

SHARED READING—REPEATED READINGS

The expert reader is able to put all three cueing systems to work efficiently. How do they do that? How do they make this complex skill look so easy, rather like the well-orchestrated symphony? With lots of practice readers develop automaticity. With very little conscious thinking they use all three cueing systems.

Think back to the novice driver, learning how to drive a stick shift. The first few times behind the wheel of a car, that young driver is concentrating only on where the foot goes, how to keep from lurching, and which gear to be in. It's unlikely that this driver is carrying on a conversation with the person in the passenger seat. Yet, with much practice, drivers are soon engaged in fluid conversation with passengers, not even thinking or paying attention to the minor details of driving. This is rather like the fluent reader, who's gone well beyond trying to figure out the grapho-phonic cues, to make sense out of what is being read. Rather, he is reading text fluently and efficiently, without paying direct attention to the sub-skills. Word recognition efficiency is developed through repeated readings. The more one reads a passage, the more likely one is to comprehend the passage.

Having children read along in a book while listening to the audio tape of the text provides both expert modeling and the opportunity for repeated reading. Students may read the passage alone after listening to the tape. Then they pair up with a study buddy to read the story as partners. This could take place in one day or over two or three days. A similar shared experience happens when the story is read first by the teacher, before students are invited to read along.

To keep motivation high for repeated or rehearsal reading, use a variety of strategies. The following strategies are enjoyed by students: signature reading, pairing/sharing, train reading, ear to ear, break in reading, popcorn reading, hot potato, and echo reading. You might prepare a chart, listing the strategies, and let students pick a different strategy each day.

SIGNATURE READING

Select a page from a story, a poem or a piece written by the student, or to increase motivation, let the student select a favorite. Students rehearse the selection aloud for rate, accuracy, and meaningful phrasing, then go out and ask as many people as possible to listen to them read. Each time they read, the listener autographs or signs the back of their page.

An adaptation of this technique is the "*Do You Want to Hear Me Read?*" notebook used in the primary grades. Each child has a three-ring binder with dividers for songs, poems, stories, and words. This anthology contains both published works and student writing. Poems and songs the children learn in class, like *The Three Little Kittens* or the *Alphabet Song*, are included along with pieces chosen by the child. The notebook grows in volume during the week, going home with the child on weekends and at the end of the year. Each time the child reads a selection to someone, the listener autographs the back of the page, sometimes including a little note. Students have been known to bring back paw-prints or drawings of their teddy bears, to indicate who listened to them. The goal, again, is to get children to spend more time reading. Students may read from their anthologies at school during the week. Think of all the signatures they could collect! One principal said she is stopped in the hall regularly by students wanting to read to her.

Do You Want to Hear Me Read?

I can read

Poems

Stories

Songs

Newspapers

This book belongs to

Dear Family Members:

Help your child become a lifelong reader. Listen to your reader, then sign your name or even write a brief note on the back of the page your student read. The children are collecting signatures to encourage them to read passages many times! If your child needs help with a word, simply read it for him/her.

Thank you!

PAIRING/SHARING

When students are finished reading a story, they put their name cards in the pocket chart. The next person in the class who finishes reading that same story goes up and takes that card back to the last reader. Then two of them find a comfortable place to go in the room and take turns partner-reading the passage they just read silently.

EAR TO HEAR/PARTNER READING

Two students are sitting side by side, facing different directions, as they read to each other (similar to the love seat position). This position for partner-reading keeps the noise level down because students unconsciously adjust their voice level to the proximity of the partner's ear. More importantly, however, is that students spend time partner reading!

TRAIN READING

Students sit in a single column, like train cars, and the caboose begins reading to the person sitting in front of him. When the caboose stops—always at the end of a sentence or paragraph—the next "car" or person picks up the reading. The goal is not to "derail" the train with any interruption, so the story is continued without any break in the passage at all. The train can go around the track as many times as necessary to complete the story. This strategy works best with smaller groups.

BREAK-IN READING

One student begins reading a passage. Any other student in the class may break in at the beginning of a paragraph or sentence. If several students break in at the same time, one gradually needs to back off so that only one voice is left reading the passage before any other students can try to break in again. Take time to practice this with students. Even though it's more difficult than some of these other strategies, break-in reading appears to be a favorite of students!

POPCORN READING

Numbered sentences or paragraphs or pages in a story are assigned to an individual or pairs of students. First, students practice their passages. Then the teacher pretends to plug in the popcorn popper, and students begin "popping up" to read in turn. They have to follow along while others are reading to know when it's their turn to pop up! When partners are reading a single page, it's up to them whether to read together, take turns, or choreograph their reading. Older students might be asked to evaluate the fluency and expression of the readings to hold them accountable for listening after they've had their turn.

ECHO READING

This strategy is important for non-fluent readers and ESL students. The teacher reads a selection first and the class simply re-reads it. Intuitively, the students mimic the inflection of the teacher's voice. The selection is usually three or four sentences, perhaps a verse in a poem. It should be long enough to force students to look at the text, not simply recall the words the teacher read.

HOT POTATO

One student begins reading a passage, and at the end of a sentence or paragraph quickly names another student in the classroom to pick up the reading. This might sound like, "It was a dark, gloomy night. Sara." Sara immediately picks up reading the passage.

CROSS-AGE TUTORING

This is a natural in a multi-age classroom. Young readers practice so they can impress the older students and, ironically, the older students rehearse the reading selection to "look good" to the younger students!

Researchers have found that these repeated readings improve rate, accuracy, comprehension, and meaningful phrasing (Beck, 1989). Researchers have also found that the old, traditional round-robin reading does not develop fluency or comprehension. You may remember the days when you sat in a reading group and the teacher said, "Let's let the first person begin reading the first paragraph and we'll go right around the group, each taking a turn." And if you were person number four, you quickly counted down to the fourth paragraph, looked at it, put your finger on the fourth paragraph and then simply waited until it was your turn to read.

Remember, it is important that students have had a chance to read the passage silently first, before moving into these activities. *Becoming a Nation of Readers* (1984) found that children should read selections silently before they are asked to read them aloud.

READING ALONE

A balanced reading program includes reading alone. Unfortunately, what *Becoming a Nation of Readers* found was that during the reading group or reading instructional time, students spent most of their alone time working on worksheets. They also found that time devoted to worksheets was unrelated to gains in reading. It is the amount of **time** students spend reading in school that is associated with gains in reading. Another recent research review (Fielding & Pearson, 1994) recommends that "...students should have more time to read than the combined total allocated for *learning* about reading and *talking or writing* about what has been read." Instead of giving students busywork or dittos during time allocated for independent practice, provide quiet reading times: DEAR (drop everything and read), USSR (uninterrupted, silent, sustained reading), NIB (nose in book), or KBAR (kick back and read).

READING TUBS

During independent reading time, students may read a book at their own independent reading level. It could be a book of their choice. Primary teachers may have reading tubs filled with books grouped by level. Use a numbering system, tub one being the easiest to read, two a little more difficult, etc. Diagnose your students to find out their independent reading level and let them know in which tub to begin reading.

Students are asked to read five books from a tub, record books read in their logs, and then sign up for a conference. The teacher or teacher helper meets with that student during conference time, selects two of the five books, and asks comprehension questions related to story structure (problem, solution, etc.). Students also read a passage from the two books. If students are successful, they are assigned the next tub. If not, they are asked to read five more books from that tub and then sign up for another conference.

Reading Tub Log		**Tub #__**
Title of Book	**Date Completed**	**Conference Notes**
1.		
2.		
3.		
4.		
5.		

An alternative strategy is to set up a schedule for the teacher to meet with each student once a week. Five or six students could be scheduled during the silent reading time each day. Record every fourth conference on an audio tape so that there is a monthly, five-minute reading selection for students to save as part of their portfolios, demonstrating their growth in reading throughout the year.

HOMEWORK READING COUPONS

To increase the amount of time students are reading, try sending "homework reading coupons." Each coupon lists several choices for reading. One school gives coupons out on Monday, Tuesday, Wednesday, and Thursday. Those students who have all four coupons returned by Friday go to one classroom for enrichment activities. Those students who are missing one or more coupons stay in a second classroom to read. For example, if they are missing only one coupon, they read for 15 minutes, then go into the enrichment room. It's easiest to regroup when a team of teachers schedules this together.

Reading Homework Coupon	**Reading Homework Coupon**
Name: Date: Please help your child notice that print is everywhere! ❑ Take a walk & read signs. ❑ Go to the store and read boxes, bottles, cartons, and cans. ❑ Take a drive. Read billboards, signs, and store names. ❑ Find print at home: on clothes, in cupboards, in TV guide. Signature:	Name: Date: Choose one activity for 5-10 minutes. ❑ I read to someone. ❑ Someone read to me. What did you read? ❑ Library book ❑ Newspaper ❑ A book at home ❑ I wrote my own story. ❑ I read from boxes & cans. ❑ Other: Signature:
Reading Homework Coupon Name: Date: As you or your child read a story, have your child: ❑ **Predict** what the story will be about; what will happen next. ❑ **Explain** word meanings and ideas. ❑ **Summarize** the story every few pages. ❑ **Ask questions** about the story as you read: why, what if, when, how, where, who, which. ❑ **Retell** the story at the end, using his/her own words. Signature:	**Reading Homework Coupon** Name: Date: Choose one or more reading opportunities from this list. Set a timer for 15 minutes! ❑ Magazine ❑ Fiction book ❑ Non-fiction book ❑ Encyclopedia ❑ Catalog ❑ Newspaper ❑ Biography ❑ Autobiography ❑ Telephone book ❑ Recipe book ❑ Other: Signature:

MORE READING STRATEGIES

RAH

The Reading At Home (RAH) program provides each student with a weekly or monthly calendar. Students choose to read silently, read to someone, or have someone read to them for 15-20 minutes. A family member initials the calendar, which goes home every night. Students place the monthly calendars on their desks each morning and the teacher walks around and stamps each initialed date box to celebrate the process.

<u>My *Reading at Home* Calendar for April</u>

S	M	T	W	Th	Fr	S
2	3 CJC ✪	4 GJT ✪	5 CJC ✪	6	7	8
9	10	11	12	13	14	15
16	17	18	19	20	21	22
23	24	25	26	27	28	29

WEEKLY CALENDAR/ASSIGNMENT SHEET

Look at the sample on the next page. In the first column students record homework assignments for the week. In the center, students record words they encounter in their reading, developing their own vocabulary lists. In the right-hand column, *My Reading Progress*, students record what they're reading and whether someone read to them, they read alone, or they read their book to someone else. They collect autographs for each. At the end of the week, students count how many autographs they've collected. *Caution: Do not set up a competitive environment where students try to compete with each other for greatest number of autographs. Encourage them to compete against themselves. Success is improvement. Ask students to self evaluate.*

WEEKLY CALENDAR/ASSIGNMENT SHEET

ASSIGNMENTS	✓	MY OWN WORD LIST	MY READING PROGRESS
MONDAY			I READ TO SOMEONE: _____ I READ TO MYSELF: _____ SOMEONE READ TO ME: _____ I AM READING:
TUESDAY			I READ TO SOMEONE: _____ I READ TO MYSELF: _____ SOMEONE READ TO ME: _____ I AM READING:
WEDNESDAY			I READ TO SOMEONE: _____ I READ TO MYSELF: _____ SOMEONE READ TO ME: _____ I AM READING:
THURSDAY			I READ TO SOMEONE: _____ I READ TO MYSELF: _____ SOMEONE READ TO ME: _____ I AM READING:
FRIDAY			I READ TO SOMEONE: _____ I READ TO MYSELF: _____ SOMEONE READ TO ME: _____ I AM READING:

NAME MY CALENDAR FOR THE WEEK OF_____ # OF AUTOGRAPHS ____

LITERATURE CLUB

Literature clubs or literature circles provide students with a chance to respond to literature, as well as opportunities for repeated reading, guided reading (from peers), and reading alone. Students may choose a book from several different selections the teacher has presented to the group or the teacher may assign books to particular groups based upon a needs analysis. For maximum participation, group size of four or five members is best. The students, reading the same book, meet daily or every other day to discuss their reading. Admission to the literature circle is by having done their homework reading. The literature group decides together what the homework reading should be for their next meeting. Students (not the teacher) take responsibility for group processing. Discussion topics include opinions and feelings as well as plot and character analysis. Another "ticket" for admission to the group might be completion of a response log in which students have already written their comments. To allow the teacher to be a member of a literature group, one group can meet while the remainder of the class is reading silently.

READING ROLES

One way of increasing accountability in literature circles is to assign reading roles. Students are given a description of the roles and their responsibility for each. Each time the group meets, students rotate roles. If the group size is five, two students may have the same role. Roles that help students become strategic readers are <u>vocabulary finder</u>, <u>story mapper</u>, <u>question writer</u>, and <u>performer</u>. Vocabulary finders are responsible for identifying new words. They write the words and the pages the words are found on, and the context clues on that page that help define each word. They then develop their own sentences using the words in a new context. In the group they call on other students to use the words in new sentences. Story mappers identify characters, setting, problem, and solution for the chapter or story. Students are given a choice of webbing the story structure or writing a summary. You might also let them choose from the variety of story structure templates provided at the beginning of this chapter. Performers select one, two, or three of their favorite pages to read aloud. This is an opportunity for rehearsal reading. It's also an opportunity for students to practice their acting talent. The performer tells the group why these pages were selected. Question writers compose questions. They may be within-text (factual), beyond-text (inferential), or opinion questions. They need to write the questions, the answers, and the pages that will give clues for finding the answers to each question. When the literature circle meets, question writers try to stump the students in the literature circle with their questions.

Question writer is often the most difficult role for students. Teach the different types of questions:

> Detail: When did the story take place?
> Main idea: Why is the title of the story....?
> Opinion: How did you feel when ... happened?
> Prediction/Inference: What do you think will happen next?
> Description: How would you describe the main character?
> Compare & Contrast: How are the two characters alike? different?
> Sequence: How would you describe the beginning, middle, and end?

Another tool to help students with this role is to teach them "Question-Answer Relationships"—"QAR" (Raphael, 1986). Begin by teaching two types of questions, those where answers can be found in the book and those where answers are "in my head." Raphael found it takes weeks for primary-grade students to understand these two categories, but only minutes for intermediate-level students. When students are ready, the category, *answers found in the book*, is divided into answers explicitly stated within a single sentence, *right there*, and answers put together from different parts of the text, *putting it together*. The category *in my head* is divided into *on my own* and *author and you*. For example, the question, "What do you think will happen next?" requires a combination of reader's background experience and the author's clues (author and you).

READING ROLES

CHAPTER	1	2	3	4	5	6	7	8
QUESTION WRITER • WRITE AT LEAST FIVE QUESTIONS TO ASK YOUR GROUP. • CHOOSE A VARIETY OF QUESTIONS: RECALL (WWWWW), PREDICTION/INFERENCE, COMPARISON, OPINION. • WRITE THE ANSWERS, TOO!								
STORY MAPPER • CHOOSE EITHER A SPIDER MAP OR WRITE A SUMMARY. • DESCRIBE THE PLOT (PROBLEM AND SOLUTION), CHARACTERS AND SETTING. • COMPARE THIS CHAPTER TO PREVIOUS CHAPTERS. • PREDICT WHAT WILL HAPPEN NEXT.								
PERFORMER • SELECT A PASSAGE YOU FIND PARTICULARLY INTERESTING TO READ TO YOUR GROUP. • PRACTICE READING THE PASSAGE ALOUD. REHEARSE! • BE READY TO EXPLAIN WHY YOU SELECTED THIS PASSAGE.								
VOCABULARY FINDER • FIND AT LEAST FIVE WORDS THAT ARE CHALLENGING OR INTERESTING. • WRITE THE PAGE NUMBER WHERE EACH WORD IS FOUND. • WRITE SYNONYMS (AND/OR ANTONYMS) FOR EACH WORD. • USE EACH WORD IN YOUR OWN IMAGINATIVE SENTENCE.								

CELEBRATING READING

Encourage students to keep track of the amount of time they spend reading or the types of books they're reading independently. For example, in the primary grades students might keep an envelope in which they keep 3x5 cards that describe each book they've read. In addition to the title and the author, they can record the story structure, mini-book reports, or use journal-type comments about their reactions to the book that they've read. The cards can be alphabetized. Students can watch their envelopes grow in thickness as they increase the number of books they read.

Early primary children can keep track of the types of books that they read by marking the appropriate box with an "X." It could be books about people, animals, toys, etc. First grade students could write the title, author, date finished, and then check which type of book.

Books about people	X	X	X									
Books about animals	X											
Books about												

As students move up the grades and you want to increase their variety of reading experiences—folklore, mystery, airplanes, space, sports, westerns, here and now, or science fiction books—let them color in a record like this:

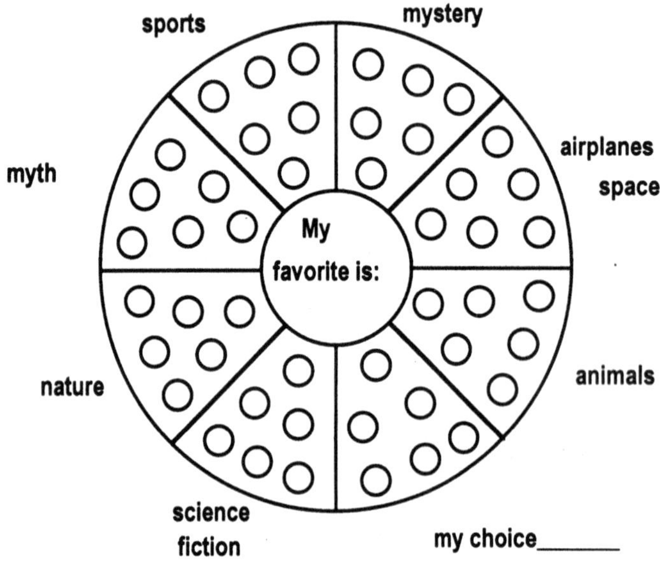

Another easy and efficient way to keep a reading record is for students to record the date, the name of the book, beginning page, ending page, and some comments about their reading at the end of silent reading time.

Reading Record

Date	Name of book	Page #	Page #	**Response Log**

WHAT TO READ

Traditionally, basal programs have prescribed what to read, and all too often, the stories have lacked either inherent structure or meaning and interest for the students. Today, as we organize our classrooms around thematic, integrated units, the "what" to read comes naturally. We select reading material that helps students with the big concepts or big understandings that we're trying to get across in the thematic unit. For example, if our theme is perspectives and we want students to understand the concept of point of view, we might select the story of *The True Story of the Three Little Pigs*. If our theme is origins, we may select books on mythology or ancient civilizations. Books or passages may be narrative or expository. The stories may be from a basal series or from multiple copies of trade books. Most important, they help develop your theme and are good literature.

This chapter title, *Reading to Read*, was selected to encourage you to allocate more time to reading...the best predictor of a child's growth in reading. Another apt title for this chapter, however, could be *Reading to Learn.* One major movement in reading instruction is to integrate reading throughout the whole curriculum. We want students to read not for enjoyment alone, but also to learn.

SUMMARY

A balanced reading program includes reading aloud to children, guided reading, opportunities for repeated readings, and time to read alone. During guided reading, comprehension is facilitated by activating background information, assisting students with grapho-phonic cues (if necessary), and assisting students with syntactical cues. Strategies such as summarizing and recognizing story grammar are helpful. Immersing students in good literature or, as one teacher put it, "marinating my students in good books" is the beginning. Celebrate reading to keep the love of books alive.

CHAPTER 4

WRITING TO WRITE

Can you imagine taking a one-year old child and testing his or her aptitude to speak? Then, if the aptitude was low, either delaying instruction in speaking or suggesting remedial work before letting that child try to talk? Ridiculous, isn't it? Instead, we know that predictable patterns for speech development emerge when children are allowed to progress at their own rate. Isn't it amazing that by the time children reach kindergarten they are mostly speaking in complete sentences and have mastered a vocabulary of over 10,000 words? They mastered this language in authentic situations where language helped them secure food or attention in a social situation. All of this happened without a single aptitude test, remediation, or direct instruction from a teacher! Learning to write occurs in very much the same fashion—if we let it.

- Writing is developmental. There are predictable patterns that emerge over time.
- Writing is a process. There are predictable stages that the writer progresses through.
- Writing flourishes when driven by an authentic purpose.

This chapter will provide concrete examples to assist teachers in meeting the developmental needs of a diverse population of students for process writing within a social context.

WRITING IS DEVELOPMENTAL

To show that *success is improvement, not perfection*, create individual writing records that document where emerging writers are in their development. Gone is the factory model approach where all students are taught the same sequence of skills and are placed in a special needs class if they can't keep up with the schedule. The developmental approach to writing begins with the child's own language and experiences as the entry point to writing (Tchudi, 1991). As children write about familiar or self-selected topics, the teacher notes where each student is, using the developmental milestones found in Chapter 1. A starting point for instruction is established by examining a child's use of:

- Mechanics
- Development of ideas
- Organization
- Style

Then the teacher's task is to use scaffolding to assist learners acquire new skills (Hull,1989). As writers participate in process writing, provide strategies to help them stretch to a higher level of competence.

PROCESS WRITING

In many respects, process is "our most important product." In traditional classrooms, process was ignored and writing was to be accomplished "on demand" or to a prompt. A limited period of time was given and all students were to write to the same prompt (e.g., "Write a description of your summer vacation. This needs to be finished before you can go to recess."). Only the product was graded. Whatever instruction occurred was focused on what the product had to have to receive an "A" grade.

After considerable study of how writers write, we've learned "...to think of writing as a 'problem-solving' process, to view it as a set of conscious cognitive and linguistic behaviors like planning, organizing, structuring, and revising" (Hull, 1989). Although these processes may not occur in this specific order, or we may engage in two or more simultaneously, teachers can focus on the processes *instead of the product.* The strategies that follow assist with the process approach.

PREWRITE

Perhaps more time is spent at this stage of the process than in any other. This is the most creative phase, when flexibility and variety of ideas are important. There are many graphic organizers to help writers *collect their thoughts.* Show how to use these organizers and provide practice with each before expecting students to use them spontaneously. Once they become familiar with them writers can select from a variety of prewriting tools to get them started on the process.

CLUSTERING

Rico (1983, p. 28) describes clustering as the key to natural writing, a "...nonlinear brainstorming process akin to free association." Beginning with a clean sheet of paper, the writer

- Puts an idea or concept in the center, enclosed in a circle.
- Spreads connections or associations out from the center circle, attaching each circle to the center circle.
- Radiates on out from the center circle as new connections are developed.

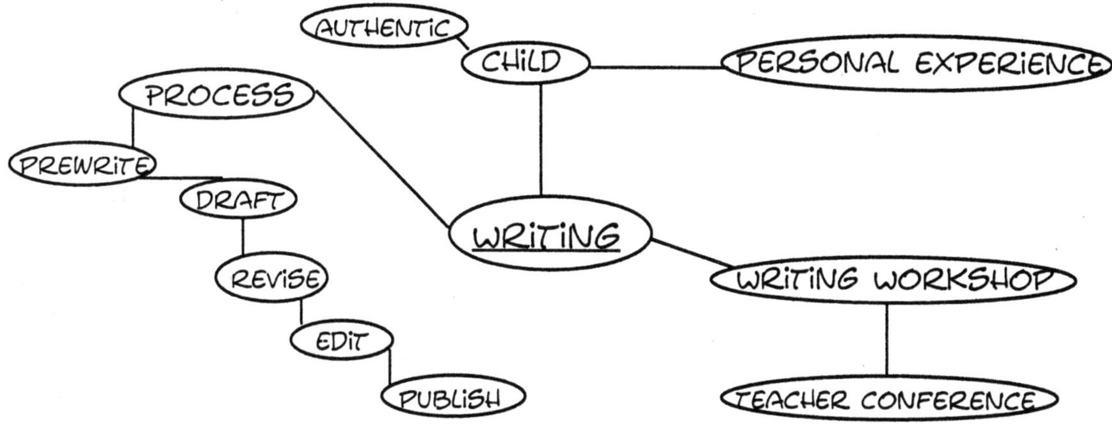

FREEWRITING

To free the analytic mind from censoring creative ideas, ask students to do a quick-paced writing to a topic (self-selected, if possible), not stopping to correct or even reflect. Tell them to ignore thinking about spelling or grammar—that's for the editing stage later.

An adaptation of the freewrite is to have writers free associate while concentrating on metaphors and analogies. The metaphor creates a new connection between an image and language. Prompts to this freewrite could be:

How would you *feel* if you were ___________(topic)?
Compare your topic/idea to a very different object.

If you're a concrete, sequential learner, the randomness of this process will bother you because there is no one correct way to proceed. Other choices for prewriting may provide more structure or appeal to different learning styles.

CARTOONING OR ILLUSTRATING A STORY

Visualization or imagery may be easier than verbalizing for some learners. On a leisurely walk or perhaps in the state between wakefulness and sleep we experience strong visual images. Many artists, scientists, and authors use these visualizations as the nucleus for their creative expression. The emergent writer will often draw first then narrate the story, not yet possessing the skills to put words into print. Even the word *imagination* contains the word *image* (to create a mental picture). Cartooning or drawing captures creative images before the writer consciously adds form.

STORY GRAMMARS

The charts provided in Chapter 3 for describing a story grammar can also be used for prewriting. Prior to using these, however, students might be encouraged to keep a continuing journal of their ideas for topics, exciting characters, settings, or problems. They can refer to this collection of ideas before putting together a story grammar.

THE W'S

WHO (CHARACTERS)	WHERE (SETTING)	WHAT'S THE PROBLEM?	WHAT'S THE SOLUTION?

Another tool to jump-start process writing is to log ideas for writing as well as to record which steps in the writing process are used to develop the idea (see "Writing Portfolio" on the next page). Not all ideas will be developed into a published product. This log helps the teacher provide students with appropriate encouragement or scaffolding.

WRITING PORTFOLIO ✍

Ideas for a prewrite:
Cluster, Web, Brainstorm,
Freewrite, Draw/Cartoon,
Use a story grammar

Ideas / topics to write about	pre-write ✍	draft ✍	revise ✍	edit ✍	pub-list ✍	genre ✍
1.						
2.						
3.						
4.						
5.						
6.						
7.						
8.						
9.						
10.						
11.						
12.						
13.						
14.						
15.						
16.						
17.						

DRAFT

To encourage writers to focus on ideas and not mechanics, some teachers label this the "*Sloppy Copy*" stage. It might be helpful to purchase stamps with the words "rough draft" or "unedited" to help parents understand this is but one stage of a long process.

Atwell (1987) suggests the following:

- No erasing; just draw a line through what you don't want.
- Write on one side of the paper—so you can cut and paste when you want to reorganize your ideas.
- Date and save all drafts and notes so you can look back at them later.

REVISE/EDIT

These stages include such activities as:

- Rethinking and rearranging ideas, perhaps adding or deleting some.
- Proofreading for spelling, punctuation, and grammar.

Peer or partner editing is encouraged as long as it is carefully taught and monitored. Provide a focus for the peer sharing. If you are asking peers to make suggestions, prompts are helpful. Post a chart with sentence starters to help editors:

PQP
<u>PRAISE</u> THE PART I LIKED BEST WAS.... YOUR POEM MADE ME FEEL.... FROM YOUR WRITING I COULD VISUALIZE....
<u>QUESTION</u> ONE PART I DIDN'T UNDERSTAND WAS.... COULD YOU TELL ME MORE ABOUT.... I WAS CONFUSED WHEN.... I WOULD LIKE TO KNOW MORE ABOUT....
<u>POLISH</u> YOU MIGHT TRY TO ADD.... ADDITIONAL DETAILS YOU COULD INCLUDE MIGHT BE.... WHAT WOULD HAPPEN IF YOU INCLUDED....

Peer Conference

Author: Title:
Editor: Genre:

Read for

Mechanics

self	peer	
❒	❒	(your choice)
❒	❒	correct punctuation
❒	❒	correct spelling
❒	❒	neat writing

Content

self	peer	
❒	❒	clear problem, solution
❒	❒	setting
❒	❒	character development
❒	❒	(your choice)

Peer PQP

Praise:

Question:

Polish:

On the following page is another tool (designed by Trudy Johnson, Saginaw, Michigan) useful for both self- and peer editing.

Pick One!

Name: ____________

Date: ____________

1. ______________________________________

2. ______________________________________

PUBLISHING

By now, our young writers are ready to go public! Set up a writer's corner where students can read their final products. A music stand can be used as the "podium". Students could choose to exhibit their products on a permanent bulletin board, "The Writer's Block." Have a basket to place pieces that students want bound into a class book. Students may want to accumulate a collection of finished pieces to have bound into a "best work" portfolio.

WRITING WORKSHOP

The writing workshop is simply the block of time established each day for writers to write! It *may* begin with a ten-minute mini-lesson, with the whole class assembled. The topic may be anything from a teacher-directed skills lesson to a student-selected issue. It may be followed by quick roll call whereby students call out what stage of process writing they will visit that day. The major chunk of time belongs to the students and their writing!

A special place in the room is arranged for peer conferences to minimize noise when students are writing. The teacher is available during this time for conferences, too. Establish a sign-up sheet to organize the process. Use a three-ring binder to record conference notes:

STUDENT NAME:

TITLE, DATE, COMMENTS	SKILLS USED CORRECTLY	EDITING SUGGESTIONS & SKILLS TAUGHT
1.		
2.		
3.		
4.		

AUTHENTIC WRITING

If writing activities are authentic, they are significant and meaningful to the learner. There is a real purpose to the communication. Tchudi (1991, p.15) reminds us that "...language is generally best learned when it is 'about something else,' whether the content be history, science, math, or one's personal experiences." To begin process writing, revisit your thematic, integrated unit. The interdisciplinary connections provide content and authentic activities for writing across the curriculum.

The following chart also provides examples of purposeful writing activities:

AUTHENTIC WRITING ACTIVITIES

CONNECTED TO READING	Response journal/log (reflections) Story grammar/structure Reading roles (question writer, story mapper) Predicting an ending to story Book report Rewriting story from different point of view
CORRES-PONDENCE	Retirement home Social issues Persuasive letter (e.g., to editor, govt. agency) Thank you note, invitation, sympathy note Friendly letter (e.g., pen-pals, relatives) Requesting materials (e.g., brochures, reports)
NARRATIVES	Personal experiences Fictional Books for younger children (e.g., coloring book with text) Scripts (e.g., plays, puppet shows) News stories Diary, journal
POETRY	Haiku, Cinquain, Couplets—to express feelings Alphabet strings Bio-poem—to tell about self Raps, song lyrics—to add rhythm and music to ideas
EXPOSITORY	Research reports Autobiographies, biographies Advertisements Recipes Instructions

Use the BINGO card shown in Chapter 5 as a motivator for students to engage in authentic writing experiences.

SUMMARY

Writing is a process. A teacher provides the scaffolding to stretch the writer's growth, authentic tasks to communicate in writing, opportunities for social interaction, and the time necessary to become immersed in the process. Students do what writers do!

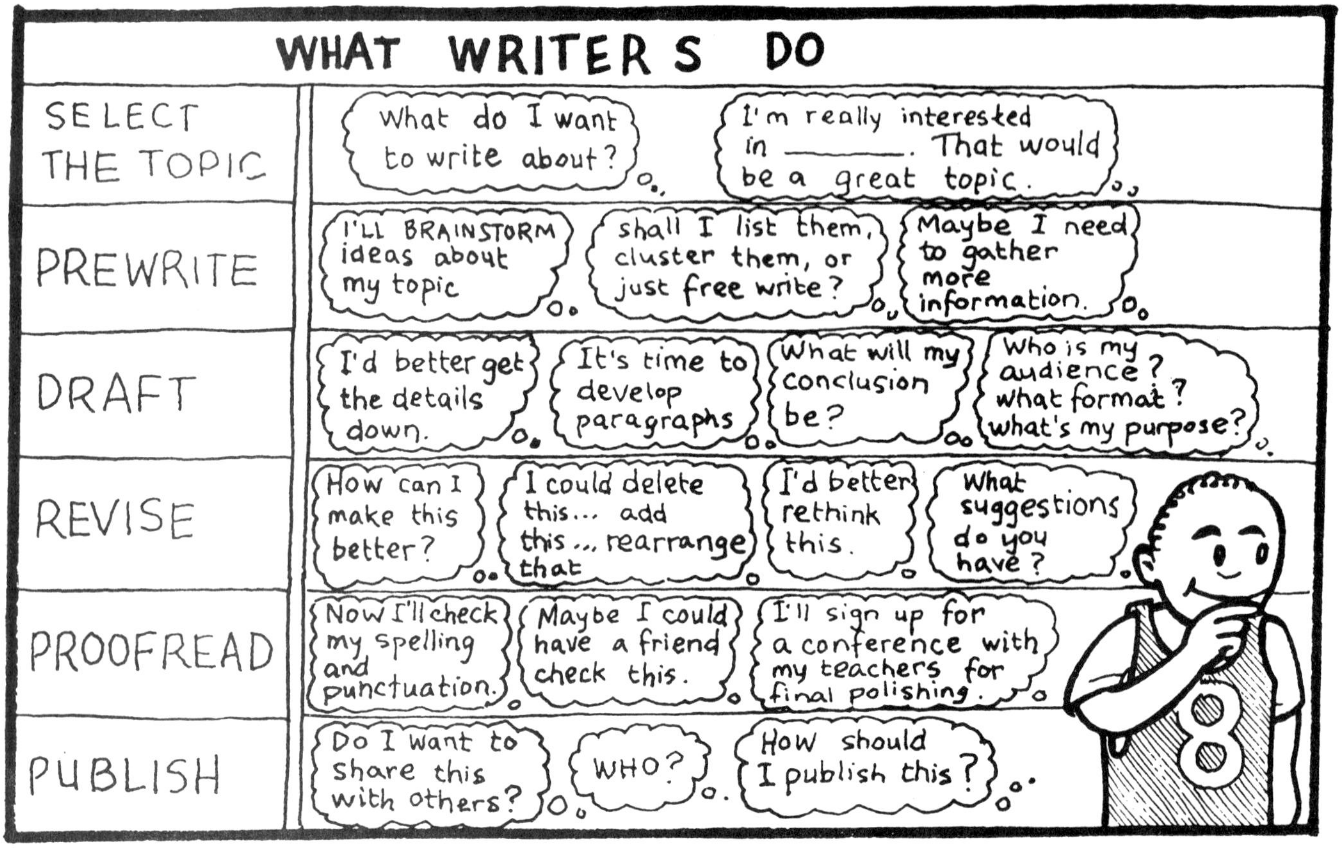

WHAT WRITERS DO				
SELECT THE TOPIC	What do I want to write about?	I'm really interested in ______. That would be a great topic.		
PREWRITE	I'LL BRAINSTORM ideas about my topic	shall I list them, cluster them, or just free write?	Maybe I need to gather more information.	
DRAFT	I'd better get the details down.	It's time to develop paragraphs	What will my conclusion be?	Who is my audience? what format? what's my purpose?
REVISE	How can I make this better?	I could delete this... add this..., rearrange that	I'd better rethink this.	What suggestions do you have?
PROOFREAD	Now I'll check my spelling and punctuation.	Maybe I could have a friend check this.	I'll sign up for a conference with my teachers for final polishing.	
PUBLISH	Do I want to share this with others?	WHO?	How should I publish this?	

CHAPTER 5

LEARNING CENTERS

Learning centers are cooperative learning in action. Divide the classroom into many small groups of one to six students, each group working on different tasks to teach, practice, or enrich classroom objectives. The activities may be at a specific location in the room or may be portable (e.g., plastic tubs carried to any location).

Chapter 1 described scheduling a multi-age classroom around three major blocks of time. The communication arts block may include a writing workshop and reading workshop *as well as* learning centers. Centers may also be used during the math block and enhance the science and social studies block as well. An integrated, thematic unit provides the inspiration for learning center activities.

WHY SET UP LEARNING CENTERS?

• One reason for learning centers is that students simply love them. When we interview students and ask them to name their favorite part of the day, more often than not it's their time in the learning centers.

• Another reason to have learning centers is purely pragmatic: You have limited materials. For instance, you may have one listening post which accommodates only six students; you may have six trade books to go with the audio cassette. With learning centers you can rotate groups of students through, six students at a time. It's also easier to arrange art supplies for six students than for thirty students.

• Learning centers facilitate lifelong learning goals. Decision making, communication skills, information processing skills, and complex reasoning are all supported. Students have the opportunity to work over a period of time, initiating and completing projects without constant teacher direction.

GOALS OF LEARNING CENTERS

There are many variables to consider in designing quality centers. As these variables are described, you'll see that there is NO ONE WAY to design them. You are the architect for your classroom. One warning, however: unless you have clearly defined your *objectives* for learning centers, students may be entertained but fritter away valuable learning opportunities. Here are some of the decisions you must make:

<u>CONTENT/TOPIC</u>
SKILL PRACTICE.......................................EXPLORATORY ACTIVITIES
THEMATIC, INTEGRATED..................................DISCIPLINE-SPECIFIC
RECALL, MINIMAL THINKING............................COMPLEX THINKING

<u>AUTONOMY</u>
ASSIGNED BY TEACHER.......................................STUDENT CHOICE
TEACHER EVALUATED........................STUDENT SELF-EVALUATION

<u>STRUCTURE OF CENTER</u>
SPECIFIC DIRECTIONS PROVIDED.............STUDENT GENERATED
PERMANENT..EVER-CHANGING

<u>SCHEDULING</u>
ONCE A WEEK...DAILY
ONE PER DAY...2 OR 3 PER DAY
20 MIN. TO COMPLETE.............................1 MONTH TO COMPLETE

CONTENT/TOPIC

SKILL CENTERS

Take a look at the many skills that your students may need to practice: reading skills such as recognizing problems, solutions, phonics; centers provide an opportunity to practice these skills. If you have a list of your district performance objectives or standardized test objectives, design your centers around these skills. Use the following checklist to record when a student demonstrates mastery at that center.

CENTER CHECKLIST X = MASTERY ✓ = NEEDS TO PRACTICE

STUDENT NAMES:														
OBJECTIVES														
VOCABULARY - SYNONYMS														
VOCABULARY - ANTONYMS														
VOCABULARY - HOMONYMS														
PASSAGE DETAILS (WHAT, WHO, WHERE, WHEN/SEQUENCE)														
CENTRAL THOUGHT (MAIN IDEA)														
CHARACTER ANALYSIS (FEELING, MOTIVE, TRAIT)														
INTERPRETING EVENTS (CONCLUSION, PREDICT OUTCOME, CAUSE/EFFECT)														
ELEMENTS OF FICTION (PROBLEM, SOLUTION, CHARACTER, SETTING)														
FORMS OF WRITING (REALITY, FANTASY)														
MECHANICS (PERIODS, QUESTION MARK, EXCLAMATION MARK)														
MECHANICS (COMMA, COLON, SEMI-COLON, QUOTATION)														
MECHANICS (PROOFREADING FOR END MARKS/CAPITALS)														
LETTER PARTS														

Skill-based centers typically involve thinking at a knowledge/comprehension/application level. The activities themselves are often completed with one visit to the center.

Flexible grouping is a characteristic of a multi-age classroom. Skills are practiced on an "as needed" basis. One way to provide this differentiated practice is by assigning centers based upon need. The student having difficulty with mechanics in writing is assigned the "mechanics" center.

This youngster is getting needed practice in zipping a coat at a skill center. Also included at this center are coats to button and shoes to tie. (Developed by Joan Boswell, Edmonds, WA)

THEMATIC, INTEGRATED

Learning centers may be used to accomplish some of the authentic tasks developed for integrated thematic units. Blocks of time are needed when students can continue to work on these tasks over an extended period of time. For example, for the unit "The Ocean & Me," students select which ocean-related group they would like to investigate. If there are five choices (e.g., Green Peace, Salmon Fishing Assoc., NOAH), each group becomes a "center." During center time, students meet to plan their investigation, carry out research, and plan their presentation. This requires planning skills and cooperative skills. Because more complex thinking skills are required, the group is given time each day for this center. Time management is important as groups must accomplish their projects within a given period (e.g., 2-3 weeks).

DISCIPLINE SPECIFIC

The unit, *The Ocean & Me*, is interdisciplinary. While students work on their projects, they are practicing math skills, communication skills, science and social studies objectives. Centers may also be discipline-specific. That is, each center may represent a specific discipline and may or may not be part of a thematic unit.

CENTERS	TABLE 1	TABLE 2	TABLE 3	TABLE 4	TABLE 5
LANGUAGE	MON	TUE	WED	TH	FRI
MATHEMATICS	TUE	WED	TH	FRI	MON
SOCIAL STUDIES	WED	TH	FRI	MON	TUE
SCIENCE	TH	FRI	MON	TUE	WED
MUSIC/ART	FRI	MON	TUE	WED	TH

At the Language Center are many games providing practice in language objectives.

AUTONOMY

ASSIGNED OR CHOICE

One important question to ask yourself is whether to assign students to centers or give students free choice. Assignment may require students to rotate from one center to the next, so that by the end of one or two weeks, they've had an opportunity to participate at each. Assignment is best when skills practice—needed by all students—is provided at each center. It's also good when centers are first introduced and you want students to learn *how to use the center.*

MENU/PASSPORT

The menu provides a perfect opportunity to break the old paradigm of all students doing the same task at the same time, given the same amount of time to finish. If you want to teach decision making, then try a menu! With a menu or passport certain activities are assigned and other activities are free-choice or optional. One extended period of time is given to accomplish everything (e.g., one week, one month). On passports students might have six to ten assigned tasks to be accomplished by the end of the month. That's their *main trail.* They have rest stops (extension activities related to theme) and side trips (unrelated to theme, recreational breaks) that they can choose anywhere along the way. This really encourages students to use their time wisely, judging how much time is needed to accomplish their main trail.

PASSPORT: <u>THE OCEAN AND ME</u>

MAIN TRAIL (one month to finish all)

1. Select one marine organism.
   a. Describe its role in the food web.
   b. Explain the effects of an oil spill, toxic spill, and oil well drilling on your marine organism.
   c. Prepare a hypercard stack (on the computer) to present your information.
   d. Write a persuasive letter to a group/company who may be adversely affecting your marine organism.
2. Select one ocean-dependent industry.
   a. Describe career options for that industry.
   b. Rank-order them from your most favorite to your least favorite.
3. Develop a visual aid to show the water cycle.
4. Read one ocean-related book from the attached list. Select one of the seven intelligences to guide your report on the book.

SIDE TRIPS

1. BROCHURE CENTER: Read brochures/literature distributed by ocean-dependent agencies. Select one to analyze: is it biased? is it objective? Add your opinion to the audio tape provided.
2. MATH CENTER: Take a break and add to our topographical, paper-mache', scaled model of the ocean floor.
3. ART CENTER: Add to our classroom mural, "Oceanic Connections."

REST STOPS

1. The water-use chart has been turned into a jigsaw puzzle. Challenge yourself: how many minutes will it take you to put it together?
2. VIDEO CENTER: Enjoy the video, "The Ocean, A Last Frontier."
3. Play the water cycle game with a partner.

One combined multi-age primary classroom (Pat Stewart/Judy Mark, Edmonds, WA) uses a combination of learning stations, a month-long menu, and small group instruction each morning. Students, divided into small skill groups, rotate through three station-times each day. A pocket chart is used to let the 50+ children in the combined classroom know their schedule. One teacher teaches a small, flexible group while the second teacher monitors students working on their menus. The menu "main dish," "side dish," or "dessert" may be a work station in the room or an independent activity (e.g.,reading a selection from a book tub). A pocket chart for the day might read:

GROUP	STATION 1	STATION 2	STATION 3
RED	MENU	MRS. MARK	LISTENING POST
ORANGE	MRS. STEWART	MENU	MENU
YELLOW	MENU	LISTENING POST	MENU
GREEN	MENU	MENU	THEME PARK
BLUE	LISTENING POST	MENU	MRS. STEWART

The BINGO card is a type of passport that might be used during writing workshop as a "rest stop" from the writing portfolio.

Writing BINGO

Try for one or more BINGOs this month. Remember, you must have a real reason for the writing experience! If you mail your product, get me to read it first and initial your box!

recipe	thank you note	letter to the editor	directions	rules for a game
invitation	order free materials	letter to a pen pal	birthday card	interview
newspaper article	short story	**FREE** Your choice: __________	grocery or shopping list	schedule
advertise- ment	cartoon	poem	instructions	sympathy card
letter to your teacher	proposal to improve __________	diary for a week	letter to a relative	book report

MATH MENUS

Marilyn Burns (1987) encourages math menus that include writing by the student to describe their thinking. For example, early primary children learning number family relationships may be given a *Build It/Draw It/Number It/Write It* Menu. Students may choose from colored cubes, paper clips, or tooth picks to "build" their families and work through each number family at their own pace.

MATH MENU FOR NUMBER FAMILIES

If the point of mathematics is problem solving and making sense of the natural environment, then we need to provide opportunities for students to do both. Through math menus, learners can explore number, patterns, measurement, geometry, probability, and logic. Instead of encountering arithmetic rules in isolation, students learn them in context while they explore math concepts and solve problems.

Following is a menu for patterns that's been used at many different levels. Students may be given a month to complete it, ending up with a book of patterns. Students work with a partner to complete the four activities for each multiple, which provides opportunities for them to use oral language as well as written language to describe their mathematical thinking. They may periodically decide to work on a "side helping" or "dessert" for variety. Frequent teacher monitoring of student progress on the menu is important to keep students from overdosing on "dessert!"

Menu for PATTERNS

Entreé for the month

Create a pattern book for the following multiples.

1 2 3 4 5 6 7 8 9 10 11 12

For each multiple:

a. Brainstorm a list of what comes in each grouping.
b. Select one item from the list. Make a T-chart.
c. Fill out a 0-99 chart for that multiple.
d. Describe your pattern.

Side Helpings

1. Make puzzles from 0-99 charts.
2. Design a game to use with the 0-99 chart.
3. Write a mystery story using multiples as clues.
4. Pick a number. List all the ways to count to that number (using multiples).

Dessert

1. Watch video: *Math, You Can Count On It*
2. Art Center: Create a multiples collage
3. Problem Solving Center

Example of lists:

Multiples of 4	**Multiples of 5**	**Multiples of 6**
1. LEGS ON A CHAIR	1.	1.
2. TIRES ON A CAR	2.	2.
3. LEGS ON A TABLE	3.	3.
4. QUARTS IN A GALLON	4.	4.
5. FINGERS ON A HAND	5.	5.
6. TOES ON A FOOT	6.	6.

Example of chart:

Multiples of 4: Tires

How many cars	Illustrate	Total tires
1	❍ ❍ ❍ ❍	4
2		8
3		12
4		16
5		20
6		24

The simplest math menu to construct is one that integrates problem solving with written language. Each week students may receive a new menu of four or five meaningful math problems. (See M. Burns materials for examples.) Students use the following format for every menu item:

1. State the menu problem.
2. What did I do to solve the problem?
3. How did I get my answer?
4. Make a T-chart or graphic to illustrate.
5. Write a *math sentence.*

CONTRACTS

Contracts provide another opportunity to combine assigned and free-choice centers. The contract shows a series of pictographs for each of the centers (e.g., sand table center, manipulative center, chart center, art center, reading tub, journal center, bulletin board center, math center, game center, easel center, computer center, puzzles, writing table, gross-motor center). Each time the student goes to a center of their choice, they color in that particular box on their contract, indicating they've been to that center. When they've used up that center choice, they choose a box that has not yet been colored. This is one way of increasing the odds that kids will try a variety of centers and not continue to go back to the same center.

WORKBENCH
ABC + ME
BOOK TUBS
WRITER'S BLOCK
PUZZLES
CREATE A BOOK
WHO
WHERE
PROBLEM
SOLUTION
CARD GAMES
CREATIVE CENTER
GLUE
COMPUTER
CHARTS
LISTENING
MATH
2 +2 4
BOARD GAMES
TRAVEL CENTER
ART
BULLETIN BOARDS
SCIENCE
BRAIN TEASERS
PEER TUTORING
THE PRIVATE EYE
YOUR CHOICE

STRUCTURE OF CENTER

PERMANENT

Permanent centers provide predictability and are easier to manage: listening post that's always set up; an art center with permanent easels and paints; a video center; a writing table for correspondence. Although the center is permanent, the task at the center may change, depending upon the classroom theme. When the classroom theme was *change*, the video may have been on seasonal change and the art center had fall leaf rubbings. When the unit theme was *relationships*, the video may have been *Cinderella* and the art center had an experiment on primary/secondary colors. Directions are posted at each center.

One favorite center for students is the publishing corner. Upon reaching the last stage in the writing process, publishing, students go to this corner to select how they'd like to present their writing. Several models of books are there: a flip book, tab book, layered book, hidden-picture book, pop-up book, trifold book, and a three-fourths book. Students get really creative as they publish a report on Washington State, using the layered book cut into the shape of the state! Or, when writing an animal story, use a trifold book cut into the shape of that animal. Or, in writing character descriptions for *The Three Little Kittens*, cut a "kitten" trifold book. Layered books make great book reports: a section for problem, solution, characters, setting, and reaction.

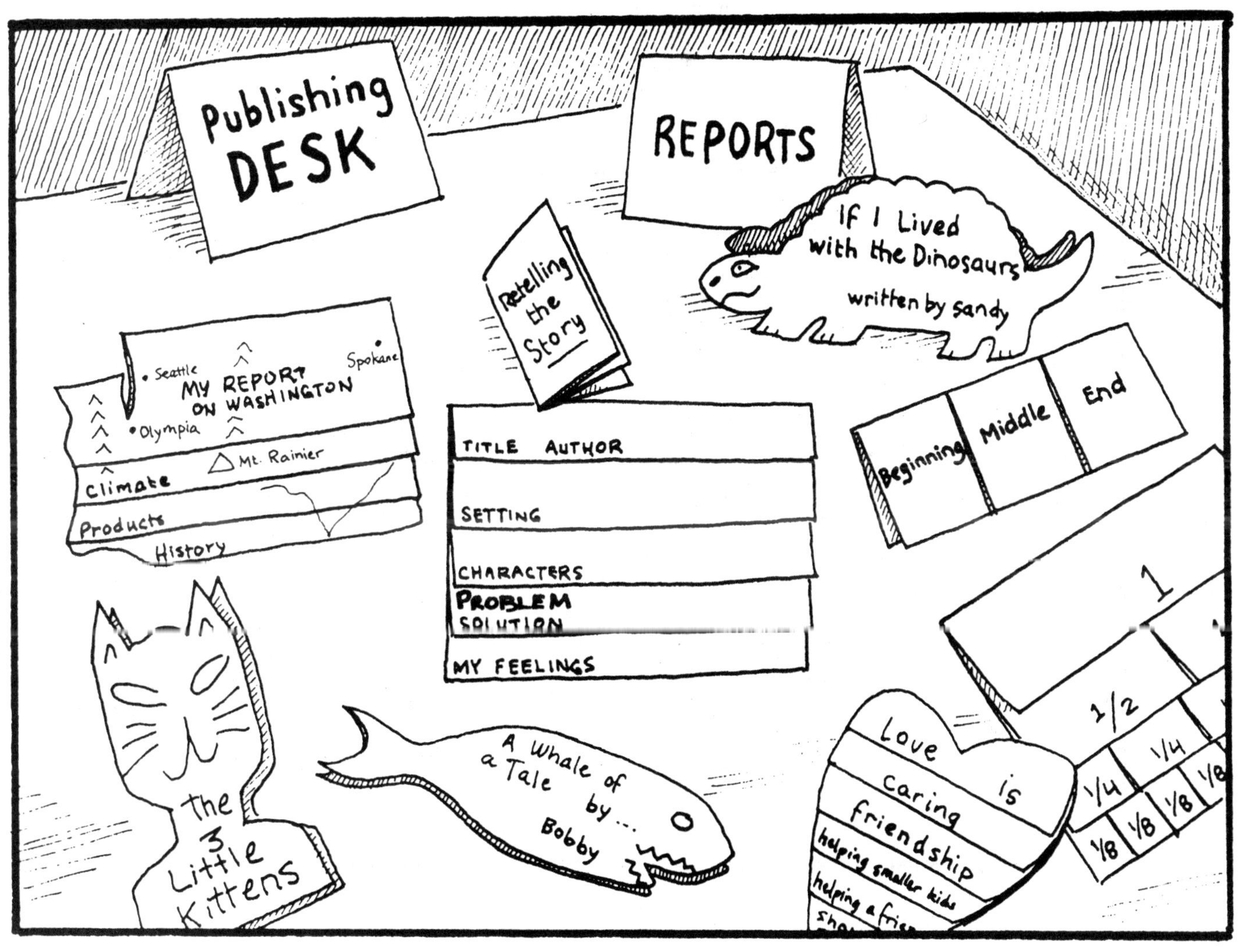

THEMATIC

Centers designed entirely around a theme or unit are ever-changing. For example, one teacher (Deby Comfort, Edmonds, WA) schedules the day before every holiday for *holiday centers*. Her class celebrated the culmination of a thematic unit on the Pilgrims and American Indians the day before Thanksgiving. She set up centers around the room related to the unit. Centers included:

- Writing with a quill pen
- Working with odd bits of leather and the tooling equipment
- Making wampum necklaces (stringing colored cereal in a pattern for beads)
- Making cornbread, churning butter
- Creating corncob mosaics

SCHEDULING

When will these centers be used? In some classrooms, students may go to a center if they finish their work early. The caution here is that students will rush through their work, doing sloppy, poor-quality work, just to get to a center. One way to reduce this risk is to be sure that there is a scheduled center time, perhaps every day for twenty minutes, to make sure that all students have an opportunity to try all centers. Some early primary classrooms have two or three center times a day.

Weekly or biweekly centers are another alternative. For example, you might have thematic unit centers every Wednesday afternoon. Using *assigned rotation*, students go to two different centers related to the thematic unit they're studying. The following Wednesday afternoon, they go to two more theme-based centers. They complete their six centers by the third week. Perhaps on Friday afternoon, students may have free choice of unstructured centers.

SUMMARY

The design and implementation of learning centers includes the following decisions: content or topic to be practiced, amount of autonomy, structure, and scheduling. A menu of activities to be accomplished over an extended period of time provides a compromise between teacher control and student decision-making.

CHAPTER 6

MANAGING CENTERS

PLANNING

Perhaps one reason why more teachers don't use learning centers has to do with time and management issues. Where do you begin? The five Ps provide some worthwhile advice:

Prior planning prevents poor performance.

Planning for six centers probably takes six times the time and effort of planning for just one direct instruction lesson! In addition to the decisions described in earlier sections, here are more nitty-gritty logistics for planning centers.

DIRECTIONS

What are students going to do at each center? If there are three steps or more to the directions for a center, put those steps in writing. With very young students, use pictographs. Remember to number the steps and write them in list format.

❐ 1.
❐ 2.
❐ 3.

If possible, usc a box for students to check off accomplishment of that step. This is very important for highly distractible students, needing a sense of direction, and it increases everyone's motivation. These steps can be written right on the passport or the menu that students are using for the month or on a chart posted at each learning center.

The degree of structuring at a center, particularly the directions, depend upon the teacher's objectives for the center. When complex thinking skills are involved, the teacher may provide guidelines for the center and let the students develop the specifics. Students may propose a schedule of completion for each of the assigned (main dish) items on a menu.

SPACE

PORTABLE CENTERS

The teacher housed in a room the size of a postage stamp is the first to reject centers: "I don't have the space!" If you don't have room for permanent centers, use portable centers that students can take back to their desks or tables.

- Plastic baggies that seal (reinforced on the bottom with tape).
- Plastic tubs with lids.
- Cardboard boxes with lids, that are the same size for ease of stacking (ask the clerk in the hosiery department to save boxes for you).

TIMING

Simply telling students how much time they're going to have at a center does not necessarily encourage productive work. They can get overly involved in one step or perhaps they can get off-task. You say "time's up" and they haven't completed their center work! Perhaps the best tool to use here is the old-fashioned kitchen timer. It's so visual that even young children can look up and *estimate* how many minutes they have left. The old Chinese proverb "Work expands to fill the allotted time," is so true, particularly when students are at centers.

CLEANING UP

This is a big issue at center time. You're most likely to get discouraged if you find that every time students finish their centers you become a custodian, picking up scraps and putting supplies away. Even very young students can be taught how to leave their center in exactly the same condition in which they found it. Have a single lesson just to rehearse sending students out to centers. "You're going to practice clean-up today. We'll only work at the center a few minutes before I announce clean-up. Then you'll show me how well you can clean up your center."

EVALUATION

Frequent evaluation of centers is necessary. Is the time being used constructively? Is the learning maximized? If, for example, centers are to provide skills practice, would students benefit more from direct instruction? Get students involved in evaluating center time, too. Try a reflection log—two or three comments about their experiences at the end of each center time.

Today I learned... This center made me feel... The best thing about this center is...

Or, ask students to rate the effort they put into the center. Design a rubric that can be used at any center.

LEARNING CENTERS: HOW'D I DO?

When the timer rings, take three minutes to clean-up and then self-evaluate your work quality and behavior at that center.

	WORK QUALITY	BEHAVIOR (INTERPERSONAL)
LINGUISTIC--"WRITE ON!"		
LOGICAL/MATHEMATICAL--"THINK IT THROUGH!"		
VISUAL-SPATIAL--"LOOKIN' GOOD!"		
MUSICAL--"SOUNDS GOOD!"		
BODILY/KINESTHETIC--"MOVE IT!"		
INTRA-PERSONAL--"DREAM ON!"		

3=great 2=OK 1=I need to improve

Another rubric for self-evaluation:

CENTER NAME	PICK ONE TO WRITE ABOUT: 1. I LEARNED... 2. I WISH... 3. I FEEL...

GRAPHICS/CHARTS

POCKET CHART

How are you going to get students out to their centers, particularly when they are assigned a rotation-type center? You need a graphical system. One easy way is to have a pocket chart made from the pockets used on the inside of library books. Put the name of each of your centers on a bulletin board and have the number of pockets underneath each center name to designate how many students should be at that center at any given time. When students enter the class in the morning, they take attendance by picking up a card with their name on it, putting their card in the pocket center of their choice. No time is wasted when it is center time; students have already made their choice. If centers are assigned by the teacher, use the stack of cards with student names, and assign students to centers based upon need.

ROTATING CIRCLE

A rotating circle is another time-efficient way of assigning centers, particularly when students are working in cooperative groups and their cooperative group will rotate to a particular center. For example, let's say you have six cooperative groups in your room and each group is named: the Circles, the Rectangles, the Ovals, the Triangles, etc. Use two concentric circles, an outside circle with the names of the centers, and a rotating inside circle that has the name of the cooperative groups. Each time groups rotate to a new center, you rotate the inner circle one notch and students can see which center they're assigned. Don't forget, however, that quick check for understanding. Before sending students to centers, say: "Read the chart to find out where you're going to go. Now, point to that center." Be proactive! Make sure that students will end up at the correct center. The transition to and from learning centers can create management problems.

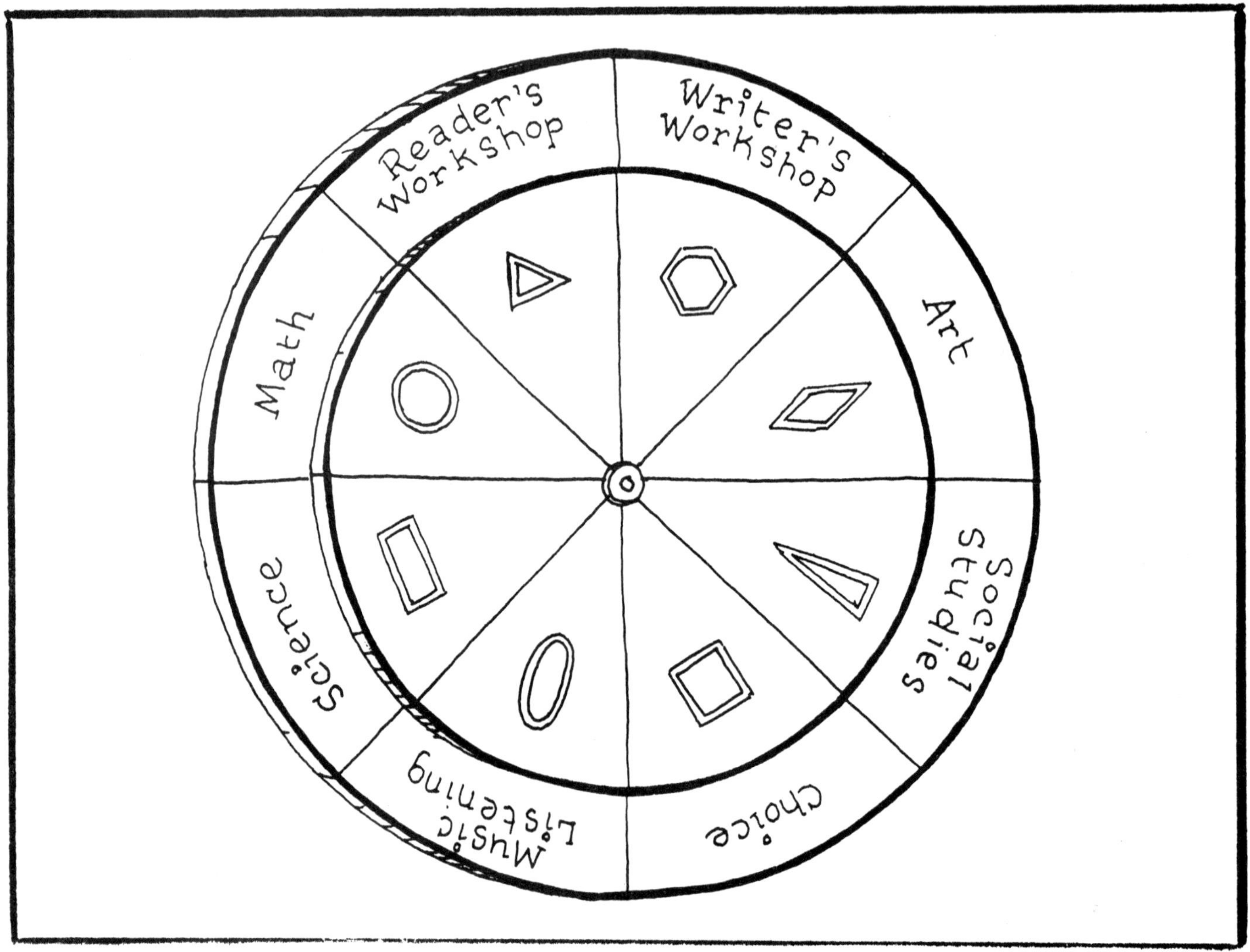

VELCRO DOTS

In addition to using library pocket cards or signs for crowd control at centers, try Velcro. Velcro circles can be used to attach student name cards at centers. The classroom pictured below (Martha Highsmith, Cincinnati, Ohio) has a math center, creative play center, ABC center, listening post, reading center, writing center, games and puzzles, a hands-on center, a dramatic play center, a sand and water center, and an art center. Underneath each center card are two to four Velcro dots. When students first go to their center, the teacher has assigned their center. When a student has accomplished his task, he signals for the teacher, or the center monitor, to come over and check. The student may them take his card off the Velcro dot, look for any other vacant dot at another center for free choice of a center. This is a wonderful combination of both assigned and free choice centers.

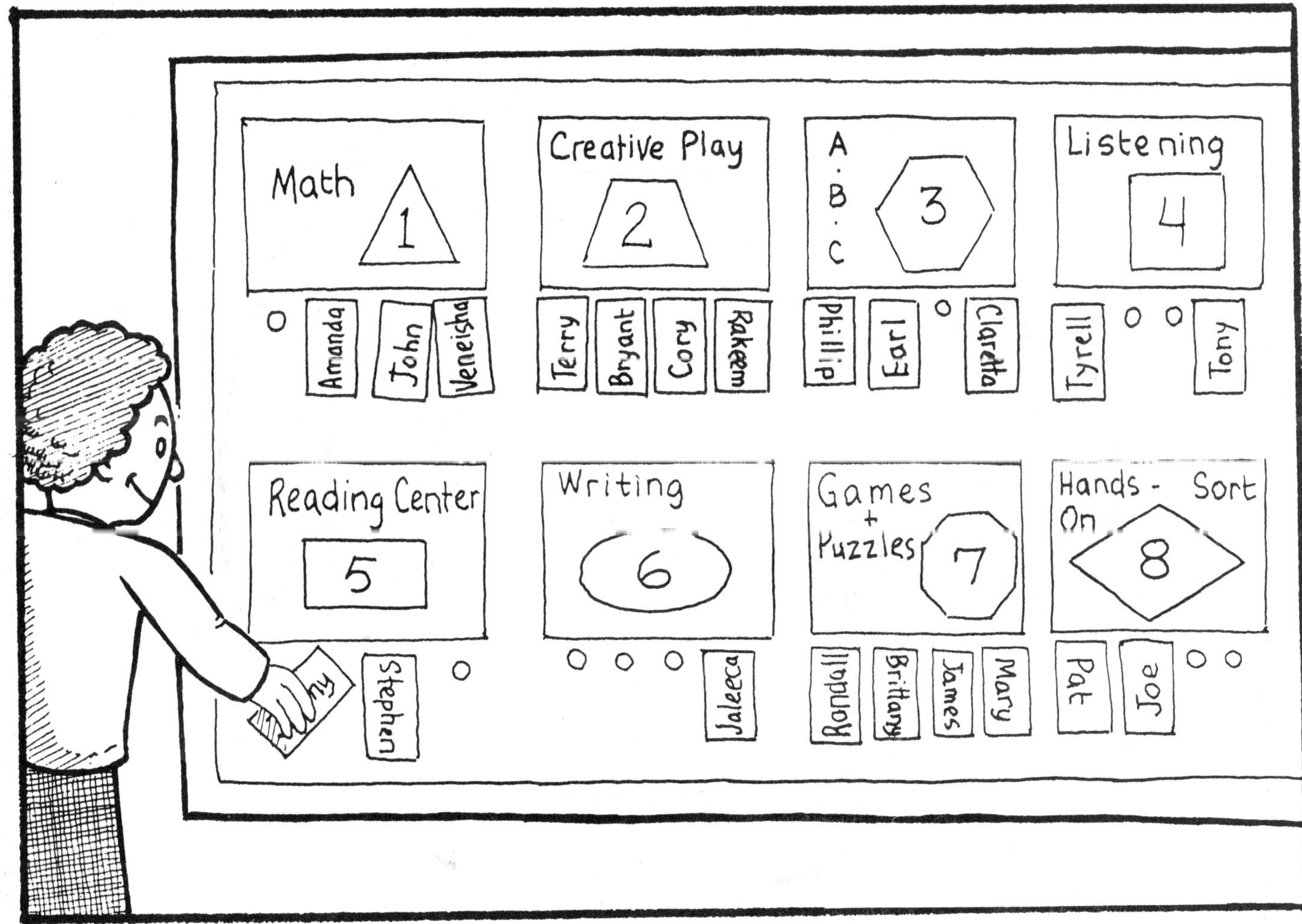

MANAGING STUDENTS

ASSIGNING STUDENTS

To assign students to groups, use some of the skills that you may have learned in cooperative learning. For example, you want heterogeneity. Consider gender and ethnic balance. Experiment with group assignments on paper. Or, put the student's name on a card, lay those cards out, and then study those names to make sure you won't have any clashes or impossible combinations. This way you can avoid management or discipline problems when you send students to their centers. Remember that group size is best when limited to four or five students. For many center activities, partnerships are best. Six students may be assigned to a center but are asked to work with a partner there.

Crowd control is critical when you use a contract or a menu with free choice. Place a sign at each center with a number—how many should be at that center.

IF YOU NEED HELP...

Something else to think about in terms of crowd control at centers is what student should do to seek help. Too often when kids are stuck or need assistance at a center, they leave their center and they come over and tug at the teacher's shirt sleeve. "Teacher, teacher, I need help!" We've probably all experienced having five or six tugging hands all at once, which tends to get rather frustrating, both for the teacher and for the students who need help. Teach students to stay at their center and signal you to come to them. How, perhaps, might they do this? You might have a stop and go sign at each center--red on one side, green on the other. The sign is flipped to the green side when students are fine and don't need assistance. They flip the card over to red when they need help. You can scan the room to see which center needs assistance. Perhaps at a computer center or writing center, have a plastic cup with the words "Help Me." Students can set that cup on top of the computer monitor when they need assistance. Better yet, when students are working in teams at a center, teach them the *three before me* routine: ask three students before asking the teacher.

DISCIPLINE

One question that's always asked is: What do I do about discipline problems during center time? Always think in terms of two generalizations. (1) Above all else, maintain student dignity. See the disruptive student privately. There's no need to shout across other students to reprimand a single child. (2) Think in terms of logical consequences. The logical consequence of not making good choices when at a center is that you lose the opportunity to work at that center that day. The student may need to work quietly at her seat on a different task.

MONITORING

Centers do need to be monitored constantly. Do "clipboard cruising" during center time. Carry a clipboard with the class list on it and take anecdotal notes as you observe students at centers. This is the perfect time to get anecdotal information for student portfolios. One way of doing this most efficiently is to have peel-off address labels on the clipboard. As you make notes about a particular child, date the notes, and at the end of the day peel off the label and insert it in the student's portfolio.

Parents make great monitors for learning centers. Send out a letter to parents, asking for volunteers to come regularly to help at center time. Type out instructions for the parents because you are often too busy to provide training when they arrive.

SPECIALISTS

If you're using inclusion, specialists may want to participate at center time. One classroom has the speech therapist work with students during center time. Another room has the reading specialist come in at center time to work with small groups at one of the centers. This makes it possible not only to eliminate the need for pull-outs, but also provides the opportunity for more students to receive special help.

LEARNING CENTERS—A PROCESS, NOT AN EVENT

Where do you begin? What does the very first day look like when centers are introduced? Think about this analogy. What would you consider when taking a group of novice swimmers to an Olympic-size swimming pool for the first time? If these students aren't used to swimming, let alone acclimated to the water, would you take them to the shallow end or would you take them to the deep end? Shallow end, for sure! In fact, you may not even let them in; you may let them sit on the side of the pool and dabble their big toes, just to get them used to the water. So, too, will we acclimate students to centers slowly, before going fully into them. Diagnose your class. If they experienced learning centers last year, your starting place will be more advanced than for beginners.

What are some of the things to think about as we move slowly into centers?

START SMALL

Consider the number of students assigned to a center. You're less likely to have problems when kids are working in partnerships or alone—team size of one or two. At the "deep end of the pool," you'd have cooperative centers of three, four, or five. Wait until the kids are ready for the larger groups.

MINUTES BEFORE HOURS

The amount of time at a center will also change. In the beginning, try to keep center time down to five or six minutes. Eventually, you can work up to center tasks that are completed in thirty-five or forty minutes, and then perhaps projects that may take two or three weeks to accomplish.

EASY BEFORE COMPLEX

Complexity of the center tasks will also go from easy to complex. When students are first learning to be independent learners and move to centers, keep the task simple, requiring low-level thinking. While no one wants to be the ditto king or queen, perhaps this is one time to use a commercially published worksheet or coloring activity that takes only five or ten minutes to complete. Your goal, that very first day at centers, is to acclimate students:

- How to read the center chart
- How to get to the center
- How to accomplish a task in a given period of time
- How to clean up the center

When students have demonstrated they can do these tasks, then increase the complexity of the center activity. Consider *process first*, then product.

LEARNING CENTERS AND MULTIPLE INTELLIGENCES

"There is nothing so unequal as the equal treatment of unequals." If learning centers provide opportunities to teach to a diverse classroom, then one filter to use to judge your centers is "multiple intelligences." Howard Gardner (1991) has written extensively on multiple intelligences. He looks at intelligence through a much broader lens than most of us are used to. Gardner defines intelligence as the ability to solve problems and make something that is valued in at least one culture or community. He argues that the traditional intelligence test to establish IQ is very biased toward only one or two of the seven intelligences. And we may be missing many opportunities to meet the needs and reach every child in giving them an opportunity to develop their intelligence.

SEVEN INTELLIGENCES

What are Gardner's seven intelligences?

LOGICAL—MATHEMATICAL

Mathematics, planning skills, formulas, hypotheses for new inventions; word problems and basic logic problems (the scientist)

LINGUISTIC

Both verbal and written; the gift of gab; reading books, writing books (the poet) (Too often this is been the only intelligence that's tested.)

MUSICAL

The ability to write lyrics for a song, to pick out patterns in music (the composer)

SPATIAL

Visual intelligence found in geometric drawings, working with images, drawings, visualizing (the airplane pilot, sculptor)

BODILY KINESTHETIC

Sometimes called physical intelligence—building your own invention from scrap materials, putting things together, hands-on (the athlete, dancer)

INTRA-PERSONAL

Self-knowledge, being reflective, doing a self-study, writing your autobiography

INTER-PERSONAL

The ability to work in groups, a charismatic individual with social skills (the teacher, salesperson) (Learning centers provide opportunities to develop this intelligence in particular.)

Armstrong (1994) suggests teaching kids about the seven intelligences. He has a pie chart of the different kinds of "smart": self-smart (knowing about yourself), word smart, logic smart, picture smart, body smart, music smart, and people smart.
The illustration below depicts children at centers designed around these intelligences.

It's not necessary to have a center for each intelligence. In fact, most tasks will develop two or more intelligences. Rather, use the concept of multiple intelligences after you plan your centers, as a filter to critique your centers. Do you provide for a variety of learning opportunities?

LESSON PLANS FOR LEARNING CENTERS

Yes, if *prior planning prevents poor performance*, sit down and write out plans for learning centers. This will help you maintain quality and establish the clarity of the objectives for centers. If centers are purely entertaining to students they may be frittering away valuable learning time. To prevent management problems, get those plans in writing. The following models of learning center lesson plans are developed for the thematic unit *Relationships*. The objective for the first set of centers is to provide practice with the social skill of making friends. The objective for the next set of centers is to provide practice with anger management.

In each plan the thematic unit is identified, the major objective for the five centers is established. A mental set, to introduce the centers to students, is planned and each center is identified in the first column (task analysis). The second column (input/model) describes what the teacher wants to have at each center—supplies, directions, details. The third column (student processing), describes student responsibilities for the center—their product or performance assessment.

The last section of each plan is a reminder to celebrate or encourage closure when that round of centers has been accomplished.

SUMMARY

The management and organization of learning centers are critical to their success. Organization includes the physical management of centers (a spectific location or portable), the visual management (signs, labels, charts), as well as record keeping and evaluation. Management of the behavior at learning centers includes teaching students the routines and expectations for appropriate behavior at centers.

Subject: THEMATIC UNIT: Relationships **Date:**

Objective(s) Students will practice friendship building strategies/learnings at centers

PROCESS/SKILL INFO CONCEPT [SOCIAL/AFFECT] THINKING SKILL

Set Give riddle: What is the best vitamin for making friends? (B-1)

HOOK TO FUTURE HOOK TO PAST ADV. ORGANIZER [INTEREST]

Diagnosis

Materials

	TASK ANALYSIS	INPUT/MODEL	STUDENT PROCESS
1.	LISTENING CENTER	Tape player; choice of taped stories: Best Friends (Cohen); Will I Have a Friend (Cohen); Sticks & Stones (Cummings); etc.	After listening to taped story, complete response log: What was the problem? Solution? Pick favorite page to rehearse & read to class.
2.	POSTER CENTER	Magazines & newspapers; glue, scissors	Cut & paste a collage of pictures showing friendship; Cut & paste a collage of words–adjectives that describe friends
3.	SECRET-PAL PUT-UP CARDS	Have names of students in can; List of 20-30 adjectives Supplies for making 3-fold cards	Draw one name; make a 3-fold book, cut to look like your secret-pal. Select one adjective for each page; write why you selected each adj.
4.	POETRY/WRITING CENTER	Chart of sentence starters for put-ups; Models of Haiku & acrostic poetry; colored paper, writing supplies	Select one format to use to write about friends; prewrite, have a friend edit, then prepare for publishing
5.	FRIENDSHIP ROAD BOARD GAME	Game board, die, story cards; for 2 players (make additional sets depending upon number of kids at center)	Pick a name; face each other; roll die; if land on star, draw card; object: game is over, you've made a new friend, when land on same space

Independent Practice or Closure

Publish a class book from poetry/writing center.
Play a class "Guess Who" game for put-up cards.
Ask listening center participants to perform their favorite page.
Put picture/word collage on bulletin board.

3-PRONG

Subject: THEMATIC UNIT: Relationships **Date:**

Objective(s) Students will practice anger management strategies/learnings at centers

PROCESS/SKILL INFO CONCEPT [SOCIAL/AFFECT] THINKING SKILL

Set This week we'll explore something everyone in this room has felt; in fact, everyone in the WORLD! What is it?

[HOOK TO FUTURE] [HOOK TO PAST] ADV. ORGANIZER [INTEREST]

Diagnosis

Materials

	TASK ANALYSIS	INPUT/MODEL	STUDENT PROCESS
1.	NEWSPAPER/ MAGAZINE CENTER	Newspapers & magazines Butcher paper with categories: traffic, world events, sports, families Glue; scissors	Cut out examples of articles/ pictures related to how people handle their anger; categorize and write your opinion of the choice made
2.	POSTER CENTER	Pictures of bugs & frogs; paper & magic markers; poster: "Frogs have it easy; they can eat what bugs them."	Create a poster to illustrate quote; somewhere in the poster, write or draw what bugs you (makes you angry)
3.	LISTENING CENTER	Tape player; choice of taped stories related to anger management (e.g., "I'm Always in Trouble")	After listening to tape, complete response log: What was the problem? What was the solution? What might be another solution?
4.	"AND THEN" BOOKS	Model of fold-a-book(legal size) Writing supplies; list of anger-provoking situations (name-calling; teasing; being left out)	Select one situation that makes you angry; write/illus. 2 "and then" books-one with good choice, one with a poor choice for handling the anger
5.	ROLE PLAY CARDS	Selection of problem cards for role playing anger management; tape recorder, blank tape	Pick one card; rehearse how you & your partner will solve the problem; tape record your final performance

Independent Practice or Closure

Post newspaper collage & posters on bulletin boards.
Play tape-recorded role plays for class.
Laminate "And Then..." books for class library

3-PRONG

CHAPTER 7

AUTHENTIC ASSESSMENT

Imagine you were told that to continue teaching in your district you had to take a test. What do you think would be the best measure of your teaching ability: *observing* you teach or asking you to take a paper/pencil test? Watching you in action is a more *authentic* measure. Before you are observed teaching, you're likely to wonder what *criteria* will be used to judge your teaching. And how will observers know *level of proficiency?* These are the issues discussed in this chapter. If we are to restructure the classroom to meet the needs of our diverse population of students using continuous progress, how will we evaluate students?

The model presented in Chapter 2 describes the design of an authentic task as the result of establishing content standards, levels of complex thinking required, and performance conditions. This authentic task can also be used as a vehicle for assessment. Actually, it's difficult to separate your record keeping from your assessment. As you record student accomplishments, you are evaluating their individual growth. Just think, if you keep good records of

- Weekly reading conferences
- Weekly writing conferences
- Learning center accomplishments

you are off to a good start!

ASSESSMENT OPTIONS

Assessment options include:

- Process
  - "kid watching"
  - conference
- Performance assessment using *rubrics*
  - debate
  - role play

- Products and projects using *rubrics, rating scales, checklists*
  - portfolio
  - journal
  - written reports
- Paper and pencil measures
  - short answer
  - visual (construct web, chart, graph)

PROCESS

"KID WATCHING"

If you believe that "process is our most important product," how will you assess it? Going back to the example of assessing your teaching, would you rather set up a specific time to be observed or tell the observers to drop by anytime to observe a natural teaching event? *"Kid watching"* is more analogous to the second example, observing students in a natural setting. To use this method of assessment requires much more organization than you might imagine.

First, decide which performance standards are best measured in a natural setting. What specific behaviors will you be observing? How will you record them? "Clipboard cruising" is a favorite method for many teachers. You'll need a clipboard and peel-off address labels with student names preprinted on them or use post-it notes to record anecdotal notes.

If you decide to record specific behaviors during learning center time, carry your clipboard with you and take anecdotal notes while you observe. If you set a goal, for instance, of observing each student once a week during centers, you can tell at a glance how many students are left to observe. Know what process behaviors you need to record. For example, observe writers *as they write.* Do they prewrite? share? take risks? set goals? revise?

At the end of each day or week, simply peel the label and insert it in a student file. A large loose-leaf notebook makes it easy to insert notes as well as add pages. Sections might include: writing conferences, reading conferences, learning centers, etc.

CONFERENCING

To develop an efficient method for student conferencing decide:

- Who decides the timing for the conference?
- What will the conference measure?
- How will the conference be recorded?

The reading strategy of book tubs, arranged numerically by level of difficulty, uses student conferencing to determine if a student is ready to progress to the next level. A white board or chalkboard is used for students to sign up for a conference when they have completed five books from a tub.

SIGN UP FOR READING CONFERENCES	
1.	2.
3.	4.
5.	6.

The teacher or parent volunteer uses the same procedure for each conference. First, select one (or, two) of the five books to use as the focus for the conference. Questions include:

- What did you like best about this book?
- Pick a selection (1 or 2 pages) that you liked and read it aloud. What is it about that selection you liked?
- What were the story elements? (problem, solution, characters, setting)

Reading Recovery specialists use a student record sheet to follow students' reading performance, noting the strategies students use spontaneously. When students need assistance, prompts are used to elicit specific strategies.

INDIVIDUAL READING RECORD		
NAME:		
Date	Book	Notes

STRATEGIC BEHAVIORS	PROMPTS
1 x 1 matching	Read it with your finger.
Picture clues used	Look at the picture.
Letter/sound clues used	Get your mouth ready.
Anchor words used	Show me the words you know.
Rereads	Please try that again.
Self-corrects	Try that again. Something's not quite right.
Reads fluently	Try reading this quickly so it sounds just like you're talking.
Takes risks when difficult	You really tried to solve that yourself. Great!

In addition to the suggestions given in the *Writing to Write* chapter for writing conferences, ask questions such as:

- What is one thing you have improved in this piece?
- What do you like best about your writing?
- What makes it the best?
- What do you like least about your writing?
- What could you do to change that?

PERFORMANCES, PRODUCTS, PROJECTS

RUBRICS, RATING SCALES, CHECKLISTS

A rubric is a tool that lists criteria that describe student performance at various levels of proficiency. It's used to score or evaluate performance tasks, products, and projects. It is valuable both for the teacher (to make grading easier) and for the student (to clearly know expectations in advance). When students receive the rubric at the same time they receive their performance task, clear targeting of behaviors enhances learning and motivation.

Rubrics for content standards (information specific to a discipline) are often set up on a three- or four-point scale, from highest to lowest level of performance. Marzano, Pickering, & McTighe (1993, p. 65) suggest the following levels to be used as a generic blueprint. Use these four descriptors to develop a more content specific rubric for students:

4	"Demonstrates a thorough understanding of the generalizations, concepts, and facts specific to the task or situation. Provides new insights into some aspect of that information."
3	"Displays a complete and accurate understanding of the generalizations, concepts, and facts specific to the task or situation."
2	"Displays an incomplete understanding of the generalizations, concepts, and facts specific to the task or situation and has some notable misconceptions."
1	"Demonstrates severe misconceptions about the generalizations, concepts, and facts specific to the task or situation."

Using these levels, here is the task and rubric given to students for the unit, *The Ocean & Me* (developed by Susan Kantor, Bothell, WA). The teacher selected a scale from 1 to 3, instead of 1 to 4, for the design of this rubric.

Project: The Ocean & Me

You've researched the position of one agency or industry with respect to the future of our ocean. You have studied the hypercard stacks designed by your peers. Prepare a position statement describing and supporting your point of view related to one oceanic problem, to be presented to a panel of outside experts.

Content standard: Your understanding of the interrelationship between humans and the ocean.
Complex thinking standard: Your ability to analyze perspectives, using inductive and deductive reasoning, and describe the reasoning behind your point of view, as opposed to others.
Communication standard: Your ability to communicate your position clearly to a diverse audience.

Rubric: The Ocean & Me

Understanding of the relationship between man and the ocean

3 Demonstrates a thorough understanding of oceanic problems and provides new insights into a particular problem.

2 Displays an incomplete understanding of the problems.

1 Demonstrates misconceptions or biased viewpoints related to the interrelationship.

Effectively uses complex reasoning strategies

3 Demonstrates mastery of inductive and deductive reasoning by identifying the elements supporting a position and articulating accurate conclusions or logical consequences.

2 Demonstrates ability to use inductive and deductive reasoning sporadically.

1 Rarely relates information gathered and position taken to the inductive/deductive reasoning process.

Communicates clearly, in a variety of ways, to a diverse audience

3 Consistently provides clear position, supporting ideas with powerful, vivid details; adjusts tone and style to the audience.

2 Position and details clear.

1 Position and supporting details not clear; tone and style not adjusted for the audience.

STUDENT CHOICE

There's an old saying that underscores the importance of student involvement in this whole process:

CHANGE DONE **TO** US IS DEBILITATING.
CHANGE DONE **BY** US IS EXHILARATING!

Just as students are more motivated when they are involved in the choice of learning centers, they will be more motivated if we involve them in the design of a task and in self-evaluation of their performance. One teacher (Donna Day, Edmonds, WA) has a class meeting to determine the criteria for quality for their next assignment. For example, the class selected: "good sentences, best illustrations, good punctuation, best you can do, good handwriting, and sticking with it" as guidelines for their self-evaluations. Eventually they progressed to creating their own project rubrics.

Older students may be involved in both designing their projects and selecting the criteria for evaluating them. On the next page is a teacher-developed project proposal form. Students in this class may propose an alternate project to those suggested by the teacher. Or, as a unit is developed, the teacher has all students or cooperative groups frame a task that is meaningful to them.

A key to the success of students developing their own performance tasks is *teaching* them how to develop a rubric for assessment. Give intermediate level students a guide to help them consider the standards of content, complex thinking, and communication. For example:

Standards **scale**	**1**	**2**	**3**	**4**
Content				
1.				
2.				
Complex thinking				
1.				
2.				
Communication				
1.				
2.				

PROJECT PROPOSAL

Name: Date:
Thematic unit: Approved: Y N

1. Describe the project you propose. What questions will you investigate? What reasoning skills will you use?

2. Provide some specific details for this proposal (i.e. how you will locate information, how you will communicate your findings).

3. Why do you want to do this project?

4. How should this project be assessed/evaluated? Design a rubric for assessment.

WHO EVALUATES?

A rubric or checklist may be scored by the teacher, by a combination of student self-evaluation *and* teacher evaluation, and/or by peer involvement. The following provide examples of each.

The forms used to evaluate creative writing, a diorama, and cursive writing (designed by Lorna Dunsdon, Edmonds, WA) are used periodically throughout the year. Before conference time, students select their best work in these areas, attach the evaluation form, and place them in their portfolios. Pictures are taken of three-dimensional projects and placed in the portfolio. As the year progresses, students and teacher together revise their evaluation tools.

The ***Partner Evaluation*** gets peers involved in assessing cooperative skills. Unless students are taught how to use this scale and the class is monitored carefully, however, there are many risks involved in any peer evaluation. This scale is also useful for literature groups. Once a week, each literature group evaluates their skills of cooperation.

Morning Madness is an example of a student checklist designed to "cure" a particular classroom problem: improving morning entry routines. Students may only use the checklist for one week, enough time to note which routines they are or are not following.

The ***Report Card Evaluation*** develops student understanding of "Personal Development" standards when they have to reflect personally on each descriptor. Teachers conference with students who need help in accurately assessing their behavior. It's helpful to have notes (from your "clipboard cruising") with specific, dated examples.

The ***Working Levels*** model (adapted by Mark Danielson, Edmonds, WA) is posted as a large classroom chart. To increase student consciousness of their work ethic, the class is periodically asked to stop their work and do a self-evaluation: "Jot down on your think pad your working level. Then, share with your study buddy why you gave yourself that rating." Or, perhaps in the middle of a written assignment, students are asked to reflect on their working level and write it down on the top corner of their assignment. This is turned in with the assignment.

DIORAMA EVALUATION

SUBJECT/BOOK:

	SELF	PEER	TEACHER
OUTSIDE IS COVERED/PAINTED			
INSIDE IS COVERED/PAINTED			
BACKGROUND SHOWS HABITAT/SETTING			
DIORAMA IS 3-D, SHOWS FOREGROUND AND BACKGROUND			
CHARACTERS ARE DETAILED			

3=great 2=OK 3=I need to improve

I AM MOST PROUD OF

NEXT TIME I WILL

CREATIVE WRITING EVALUATION

I am proud of this. I know I can always get better. Here are the points I would give myself:

	ME	TEACHER
I WROTE AS I TALK.		
I WENT INTO DETAIL (ELABORATED). NO: I GOT A BIKE. YES: I GOT A NEW, RED, SHINY BIKE.		
MY IDEAS ARE INTERESTING AND ORIGINAL.		
I HAVE A BEGINNING, MIDDLE, AND END.		
I PUT IN PERIODS AND CAPITALS.		
I WROTE NEATLY.		

3=great 2=OK 1=I need to improve

THIS IS WHAT I WANT TO IMPROVE:

CURSIVE EVALUATION

	I need to improve	OK	Great!
MY NEW LETTERS ARE MADE CORRECTLY.			
MY OLD LETTERS ARE MADE CORRECTLY.			
I HAVE NO SINKERS OR FLOATERS.			
MY SPACING IS GOOD.			
MY CURSIVE IS NEAT.			

TOTAL POINTS POSSIBLE:
MY TOTAL POINTS EARNED:

PRINTING EVALUATION

	YES	NO
I printed from left to right. go → stop		
I made straight sticks. |||		
I made round balls.		
I made the letters touch the ceiling and the floor. Aa		
I made finger spaces between words. is he		
I pressed lightly.		

I did beautiful work. I tried hard. I raced.

PARTNER EVALUATION

MY NAME: PARTNER:

	Needs to improve	OK	Great!
MY PARTNER WAS ON TASK.			
MY PARTNER CHECKED MY WORK.			
MY PARTNER USED A QUIET VOICE.			
MY PARTNER TOOK TURNS.			
MY PARTNER COOPERATED.			

WHAT MY PARTNER DID WELL:

NEXT TIME MY PARTNER COULD IMPROVE BY:

MORNING MADNESS

DID I REMEMBER? ✓

	MON	TUES	WED	THUR	FRI
COAT ON COATRACK					
LUNCH ARRANGEMENTS					
HOMEWORK READY					
PENCIL SHARPENED					
ENTRY TASK COMPLETED					

REPORT CARD EVALUATION

THESE ARE THE AREAS OF PERSONAL DEVELOPMENT TO BE EVALUATED ON YOUR REPORT CARD. PLEASE SELF-EVALUATE TO HELP ME WITH THE FINAL.

WEEK	1	2	3	4	5	6	7	8
DO YOU LISTEN ATTENTIVELY?								
DO YOU FOLLOW DIRECTIONS?								
DO YOU COMPLETE YOUR ASSIGNMENTS ON TIME?								
DO YOU WORK NEATLY?								
DO YOU WORK INDEPENDENTLY WHEN ASKED TO?								
DO YOU SHOW CONSIDERATION AND RESPECT FOR OTHERS?								
DO YOU PRACTICE GOOD SPORTSMANSHIP?								
DO YOU SHOW RESPECT FOR SCHOOL PROPERTY?								
DO YOU STAY ON TASK?								
ARE YOU ORGANIZED?								

3=GREAT! 2=OK 1=I NEED TO IMPROVE

WORKING LEVELS

LEVEL 4 GETS WORK DONE, ACTS RESPECTFULLY, WORKS WITH OTHERS WHEN NEEDED.

LEVEL 3 GETS WORK DONE
ACTS RESPECTFULLY

LEVEL 2 WORKS WHEN REMINDED

LEVEL 1 NOT WORKING

LEVEL 0 KEEPS OTHERS FROM WORKING

PORTFOLIOS

Once teachers begin using portfolios to celebrate student growth in learning, they wonder why it took them so long to try them! If you're just beginning, here are a few things to consider:

WHAT IS THE PURPOSE?

Will portfolios be shared with parents? peers? other teachers? Will they showcase "best works," be a working or progress portfolio, or be used for teacher assessment purposes? If you decide upon all three purposes, consider how to manage them:

- Color code each type of portfolio.
- Provide a different storage place for each.
- Assign a student number (based upon alphabetized class list), so folders can be found and returned quickly.
- Consider the transition to/from the portfolio box; would it be easier to dismiss students by table to get their folders?
- Expanding file folders are necessary if you include bulky items such as audio tapes of student reading.

SELECT CONTENTS OF PORTFOLIO

If students select the pieces to be included, ask them to include a reflection slip that describes why they selected this particular piece. Or, teacher and student together may decide upon which pieces to include. As the year progresses, the items included should demonstrate student *growth*. Celebrate the slogan *Success is improvement, not perfection!* Portfolios measure a child only against his or her own past performance. They *allow* for diversity in the classroom!

SCHEDULE A TIME TO REVIEW PORTFOLIOS

Review portfolios when students are adding to them as well as when you want to interview students about their portfolio. You may want to even schedule a *portfolio swap*, when students trade with a study buddy. This provides a wonderful opportunity for students to practice giving put-ups (compliments).

Don't forget to include parents in the portfolio review! Use a weekly "Boomerang" folder in which work for the week is sent home for parent review. Working with their child, parents select one piece to be returned to school and placed in the working portfolio.

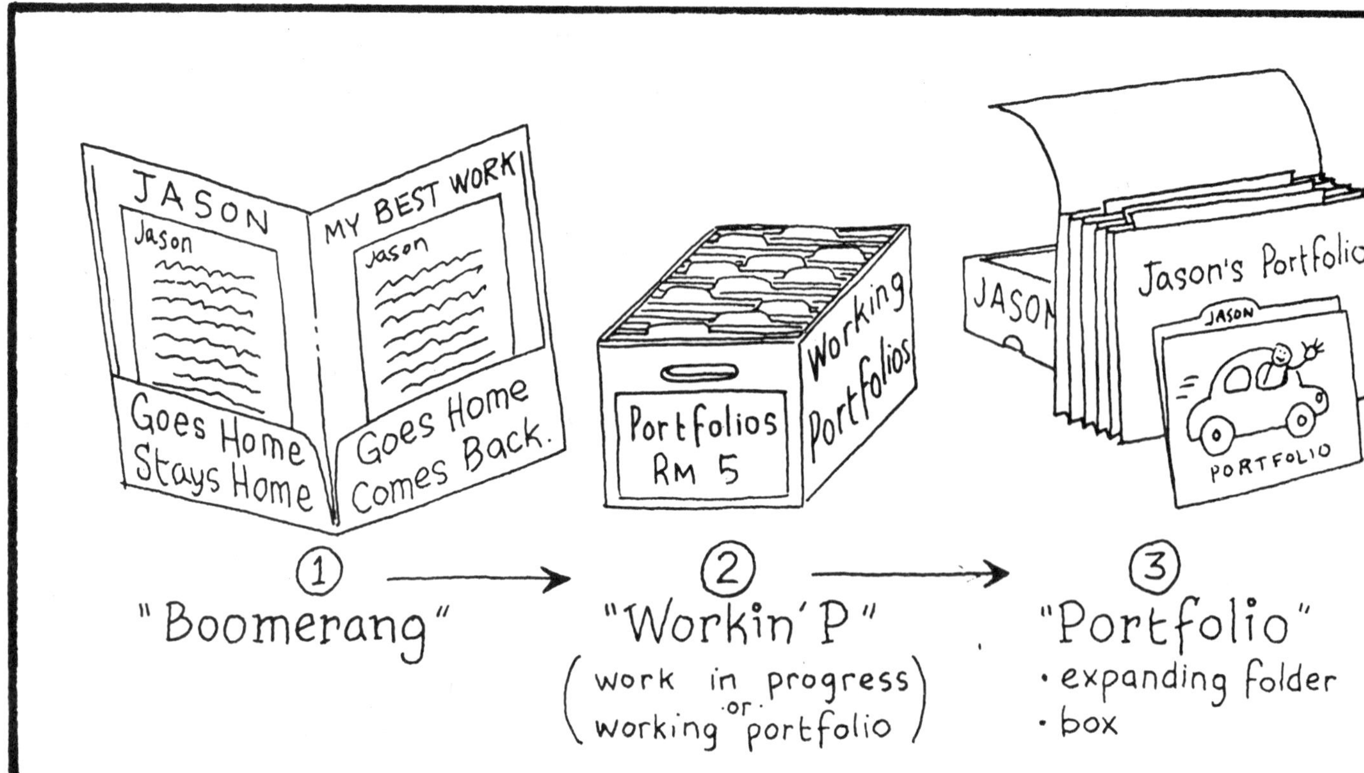

TEACH STUDENTS HOW TO SELF-REFLECT

This should be going on throughout the school year, not only at the time portfolio items are selected. A *ticket-out-the-door* might include questions like these:

- What did you do today that really made you think?
- What can you do this month that you couldn't do last month?
- What could you improve?

When students select work from their *working* portfolios to place in their *best works* folders, they should write a reflective piece.

- Choose a piece that makes you feel proud. Explain why you are proud of it more than some of your other work.
- Choose a piece that shows growth or improvement in your work. Explain what or how you have improved.
- Choose a piece of work that was a challenge for you to complete. Explain what about it was the hardest for you.

PAPER AND PENCIL MEASURES

Yes, there is still a place for multiple choice and short answer tests. Yet, with the changes districts have made in describing educational goals, these are less viable. The SCANS report (*What Work Requires of Schools*, Dept. of Labor, 1991) recommends competencies in:

- Resources (i.e., organizes time, evaluates performance)
- Interpersonal skills (i.e., participates as a member of a team, works with diversity)
- Information processing
- Use of technology
- Systems (i.e., understands complex inter-relationships)

It's impossible to measure competence in these areas with a paper and pencil measure!

Perhaps the biggest problem facing teachers now is that lag between what districts are using as test measures and the performance standards developed. Do they prepare students to take standardized tests on isolated skills or prepare students for process writing or reading for meaning?

SUMMARY

The changes in assessment over the past decade have shaped the tools we are using today as an integral part of the teaching/learning process. Instead of developing a test *after* writing and teaching the lessons, the tasks/practice activities we design for students *during* the lessons have become the assessment tasks.

Good teaching is measured not by what the teacher does in the classroom, but rather by what the students are doing! Authentic assessment measures these student behaviors:

- The products they produce
- The process they use
- The performances they give

Instead of a test full of surprises at the end of a unit, students are given a rubric or scale that specifically describes standards for excellence *at the beginning of the unit.* Process as well as product is measured. Students are encouraged to take responsibility for their learning by becoming involved in the assessment process—through self-evaluation.

CONCLUDING NOTE

FROM A COGNITIVE PERSPECTIVE, IT'S NOT ENOUGH TO RECEIVE INFORMATION—YOU NEED TO CONSTRUCT MEANING. ANSWER THE FOLLOWING QUESTIONS—INTERPRET YOUR READING AND LOOK FOR CONNECTIONS.

1. WHAT IS THE RELATIONSHIP BETWEEN AN INTEGRATED, THEMATIC UNIT AND READING/WRITING INSTRUCTION? ...MATH/SCIENCE/SOCIAL STUDIES INSTRUCTION?

2. HOW DOES AN INTEGRATED, THEMATIC UNIT INFLUENCE LEARNING CENTERS? ...THE USE OF A MENU/PASSPORT?

3. WHAT SPECIFIC READING AND WRITING STRATEGIES WILL HELP YOU ACCOMMODATE DIVERSITY IN YOUR CLASSROOM?

4. HOW DO LEARNING CENTERS HELP TO PROVIDE DEVELOPMENTALLY APPROPRIATE PRACTICE?

5. HOW CAN THE APPROACH TO ASSESSMENT DESCRIBED IN THIS TEXT ASSIST YOU IN EVALUATING STUDENTS' UNEVEN DEVELOPMENT IN THE DIVERSE CLASSROOM?

6. IN A MODEL SCHOOL, PROVIDING DEVELOPMENTALLY APPROPRIATE PRACTICES AND CONTINUOUS PROGRESS FOR ALL LEARNERS, WHAT INSTRUCTIONAL STRATEGIES MIGHT YOU OBSERVE IN CLASSROOMS? (SOME HINTS ARE LISTED BELOW.)

HOME BASE	ENTRY TASK; JOURNAL WRITING; MORNING NEWS, GOAL SETTING & DAILY SCHEDULE; SOCIAL SKILL INSTRUCTION
COMMUNICATION ARTS	SHARED READING; READING WORKSHOP—READERS' CHOICE, TEACHER CONFERENCING; LITERATURE CIRCLES; RESPONSE LOGS; READING TO STUDENTS; WRITING WORKSHOP—MINI-LESSONS, TEACHER & PEER CONFERENCING, PROCESS WRITING
MATH	COOPERATIVE LEARNING; MATH MENUS; TEACHER-DIRECTED LESSONS; LEARNING CENTERS
SOCIAL STUDIES/ SCIENCE	THEMATIC LEARNING CENTERS; COOPERATIVE GROUPS; PROJECTS; MENUS; TEACHER-DIRECTED LESSONS; AUTHENTIC READING & WRITING ACTIVITIES
HOME BASE	SELF & GROUP EVALUATION; HOMEWORK PLANNING; PORTFOLIO REVIEW

REFERENCES

Adams, M. (1990). *Beginning to Read: Thinking and Learning about Print. (A Summary)* Urbana-Champaign, IL: Center for the Study of Reading, The Reading Research and Education Center.

Anderson, R. & B. Pavan (1993). *Nongradedness: Helping It to Happen.* Lancaster, PA: Technomic Publishing Co.

Armstrong, T. (1994). *Multiple Intelligences in the Classroom.* Alexandria, VA: Assoication for Supervision and Curriculum Development.

Atwell, N. (1987). *In the Middle: Writing, Reading, and Learning with Adolescents.* Portsmouth, NH: Heinemann.

Beck, I. (1989). "Improving Practice Through Understanding Reading." In *Toward the Thinking Curriculum: Current Cognitive Research.* Alexandria, VA: Association for Supervision and Curriculum Development.

Becoming a Nation of Readers: The Report of the Commission on Reading. (1984). Washington, DC: The National Institute of Education.

Brophy, J. & J. Alleman (1991). "A Caveat: Curriculum Integration Isn't Always a Good Idea." *Educational Leadership* 49(2): 66.

Burns, M. (1987). *A Collection of Math Lessons from Grades 3 through 6.* White Plains, NY: Math Solutions Publications.

Caine, R. & G. Caine (1991). *Making Connections: Teaching and the Human Brain.* Alexandria, VA: Association for Supervision and Curriculum Development.

Fielding, L. and P. Pearson (1994). "Synthesis of Research: Reading Comprehension: What Works." *Educational Leadership* 51(5): 62-68.

Gardner, H. (1991). *The Unschooled Mind: How Children Think & How Schools Should Teach.* New York: Basic Books, Inc.

Gardner, H. (1993). *Multiple Intelligences.* New York. Basic Books, Inc.

Grant, J. (1993). "The Multiage-Continuous Progress Children's Bill of Rights." In *Multiage Classrooms: The Ungrading of American's Schools.* Peterborough, NH: The Society for Developmental Education.

Haberman, M. (1991). "The Pedagogy of Poverty Versus Good Teaching." *Phi Delta Kappan* December: 290-294.

Hull, G. (1989). "Research on Writing: Building a Cognitive and Social Understanding of Composing." In *Toward the Thinking Curriculum: Current Cognitive Research.* Alexandria, VA: Association for Supervision and Curriculum Development.

Jacobs, H. (1989). "The Interdisciplinary Model: A Step-by-Step Approach for Developing Integrated Units of Study." In *Interdisciplinary Curriculum: Design and Implementation,* edited by H. Jacobs. Alexandria, VA: Association for Supervision and Curriculum Development.

Marzano, R., D. Pickering, & J. McTighe (1993). *Assessing Student Outcomes.* Alexandria, VA: Association for Supervision and Curriculum Development.

Newmann, F. & G., Wehlage (1993). "Five Standards of Authentic Instruction." *Educational Leadership* 50(7): 8-12.

Perkins, D. (1989). "Selecting fertile themes for integrated learning." In *Interdisciplinary Curriculum: Design and Implementation,* edited by H. Jacobs. Alexandria, VA: Association for Supervision and Curriculum Development.

Raphael, T. (1986). "Teaching Question Answer Relationships, revisited." *The Reading Teaching*, February: 516-522.

Rico, G. (1983). *Writing the Natural Way.* Los Angeles: J.P. Tarcher, Inc.

Roth, K. (1994). "Second Thoughts About Interdisciplinary Studies." *American Educator,* Spring: 44-48.

Routman, R. (1991). *Invitations.* Portsmouth, NH: Heinemann.

Slavin, R. & N. Madden (1989). "What Works for Children at Risk: A Research Synthesis." *Educational Leadership* 46(5): 4-13.

Stanovich, K. (1994). "Romance and reality." *The Reading Teacher,* 47(4): 280-289.

Tchudi, S. (1991). *Planning and Assessing the Curriculum in English Language Arts.* Alexandria, VA: Association for Supervision and Curriculum Development.

The Nongraded Primary: Making Schools Fit Children (1992). Arlington, VA: American Association of School Administrators.

Wiggins, G. (1995). "Curricular Coherence and Assessment: Making Sure That the Effect Matches the Intent." In *Toward a Coherent Curriculum*, edited by J. Beane. Alexandria, VA: Association for Supervision and Curriculum Development.

INDEX

~ NOTES ~

~ NOTES ~

~ NOTES ~